No Salt, No Sugar, No Fat

Revised Edition

Jacqueline Williams
Goldie Silverman

BRISTOL PUBLISHING ENTERPRISES
Hayward, California

Printed in the United States of America.

ISBN 1-55867-306-7

Cover design: Frank J. Paredes
Cover photography: John A. Benson
Food styling: Randy Mon
Illustrator: Carol Webb Atherly

CONTENTS

1 Introduction to the Third Edition
3 It's All in the Label
7 Useful Staples
18 A Few of Our Favorite Things
20 Appetizers and Snacks
36 Breakfast
51 Beans
63 Beef
73 Chicken
90 Seafood
105 Soups
116 Vegetables
129 Grains
138 Desserts
150 A Note on the Nutritional Information
151 Index

INTRODUCTION TO THE THIRD EDITION

Before personal health concerns forced us to change our diets, we, like everyone else we knew, had often been eating meat twice a day, nibbling cheeses and fried snacks between meals, flavoring our salads and vegetables with oil or creamy dressings, and sweetening desserts with nothing but sugar. Cookbooks told us how to brown in fat, season to taste with salt, and start most dessert recipes by creaming butter and sugar together. There was not much help for the cook trying to cope with a low-fat, low sodium, low cholesterol, reduced sugar diet. If we wanted to eat that way, we discovered, we would have to develop new techniques and new recipes ourselves.

We began to work on the first edition of NO SALT, NO SUGAR, NO FAT in 1978. People laughed at our idea for a book and said, No fat, no fun, no taste, but we persevered. Armed with a notebook and grocery list, we investigated the supermarket shelves to see what, if any, low-fat, low sodium, low sugar foods were available. There weren't many! Unsweetened juice concentrates were limited to apple, orange and pineapple flavors. Sugar-free jams were loaded with artificial ingredients. Breads, cereals and crackers came burdened with fat, sugar and salt. Sapsago cheese, a hard, green, smelly lump, was the only nonfat cheese available, and it was high in sodium. Canned beans were usually cooked in lard and canned soups were heavily salted. Those who wanted lean ground beef or turkey had to grind it themselves.

We concluded that almost everything for the low-fat, low-salt kitchen would have to be made from scratch. In our first edition of NO SALT, NO SUGAR, NO FAT we suggested that our readers set aside a few hours every week to prepare beans cooked without salt; nonfat yogurt; unsalted, defatted stocks and sauces; and salt-free salsa and seasoning blends.

What a difference fifteen years makes! Now there are multiple brands of nonfat and low-fat cheeses, yogurt, salad dressings, cholesterol-free egg substitutes, and even sour cream alternatives. Low sodium or no-salt-added canned tomatoes, beans, soups and other vegetables fill the supermarket shelves. Juice concentrates come in many exotic combinations, joined by different flavored all-fruit sweeteners. There is even a fruit-sweetened chocolate sauce made without added fat or sugars. Corn and potato chips come baked, not fried; nonfat crackers, cookies and bakery products proliferate; oil-free popcorn can be prepared in the microwave, air-popped or bought already popped; and the salt on pretzels has been left in the salt shaker. There are so many salt-free shake-on flavoring blends that it is hard to choose which one to buy. The completely lazy cook can even buy low-fat, low sodium TV dinners.

It was time to revise NO SALT, NO SUGAR, NO FAT.

IT'S ALL IN THE LABEL

Learn to read labels. Labels enable people to know the nutritional value of the foods they are buying. After years of wrangling between different government agencies, new labeling regulations have been standardized so that consumers can easily compare the many brands of foods that they confront on the supermarket shelves. Labels should list the total fat and calories per serving, and compare these to a maximum recommended amount in a daily diet of 2000 calories. Labels will also list and compare the amounts of cholesterol, saturated fat, sodium, and total carbohydrate.

Here are some of the other terms you may encounter on the back of the package:

LOW-FAT: A food so labeled must meet two criteria. A serving of food can not have more than 3 grams of fat, and 50 grams of the food must have less than 3 grams of fat. (The second requirement ensures that foods where the usual serving is quite small, for example nondairy creamer, cannot be called low-fat.)

LIGHT: A food so labeled must contain 50% less fat or $1/3$ fewer calories than the original food to which it is being compared. If the food is also reduced in sodium by 50%, it could be described as light in salt, but it cannot be called light in salt if it is not also reduced in fat and/or calories.

THE REVISED NUTRITION FACTS LABEL

THIS IS A SAMPLE LABEL FOR MACARONI AND CHEESE FROM THE FDA

1. Look first at the serving size: it is important you know how many servings you are consuming. If you eat double the suggested serving size, you consume twice the calories, fat and other nutrients shown on the label.

2. The calorie section of the label can help you manage your weight. Remember that the number of servings you consume determines the number of calories you actually eat. In general, 40 calories is low; 100 calories is moderate; 400 calories or more is high.

3. The nutrients listed first on the label (fat, cholesterol and sodium) are the ones Americans generally eat in adequate amounts, or even too much. You need to monitor your intake of these nutrients carefully.

4. The second shaded group of nutrients (dietary fiber, vitamin A, vitamin C, calcium and iron) are ones Americans do not always get enough of.

Nutrition Facts

Serving Size 1 cup (228g)
Servings Per Container 2

Amount Per Serving

Calories 250   Calories from Fat 110

	% Daily Value*
Total Fat 12g	18%
Saturated Fat 3g	15%
Trans Fat 3g	
Cholesterol 30mg	10%
Sodium 470mg	20%
Total Carbohydrate 31g	10%
Dietary Fiber 0g	0%
Sugars 5g	
Protein 5g	

Vitamin A	4%
Vitamin C	2%
Calcium	20%
Iron	4%

* Percent Daily Values are based on a 2,000 calorie diet. Your Daily Values may be higher or lower depending on your calorie needs.

	Calories:	2,000	2,500
Total Fat	Less than	65g	80g
Sat Fat	Less than	20g	25g
Cholesterol	Less than	300mg	300mg
Sodium	Less than	2,400mg	2,400mg
Total Carbohydrate		300g	375g
Dietary Fiber		25g	30g

Less and **reduced**: The terms are now synonymous, and to make the claim there must be a reduction of at least 25% of the nutrient, and the actual percentage of the reduction must be listed. Example: 50% less fat.

SUGAR, SUGAR EVERYWHERE

Commonly eaten sugars and sweeteners do not provide any health benefits; they simply load the body with excessive calories. Be aware that sugar may be listed on the ingredient list of a label in many different ways: as sucrose, glucose, fructose, corn syrup, corn sweeteners, maltose, dextrose, sugar, honey or juice concentrates.

Natural sweeteners such as fruits and vegetables supply vitamins, minerals and fiber as well as sweet taste. We have chosen to sweeten with juice concentrates or all-fruit spreads; although they are not as nutritious as fresh or frozen fruits, they do offer small amounts of nutrients and a more complex flavor than simple sugars.

FACTS ABOUT FAT

All fats, liquid or solid, saturated or unsaturated, provide 9 calories per gram of fat. Every time you use 1 tablespoonful of any kind of fat, you use 13.6 grams of fat or 122 fat calories. But some kinds of fat are less desirable than others. Persons who consume too much saturated fat tend to have too much cholesterol in their bloodstreams. Diets low in saturated fat seem to help reduce the amounts of cholesterol in the body.

The new label will show you the total grams of fat in a product, the grams of saturated fats and cholesterol, and also the amounts of each of these you should consume in one day. Use this information to choose food wisely.

PLEASE DON'T PASS THE SALT

Salt is sodium chloride. Sodium is the ingredient we are trying to avoid. Sodium bicarbonate, sodium benzoate, disodium phosphate and monosodium glutamate are all names on labels indicating that sodium is present.

Formerly, food manufacturers were not required to list the amount of sodium in a product; under the new labeling rules, they must! Furthermore, terms describing sodium are defined by law. "Sodium free" means less than 5 milligrams per serving; "very low sodium," means less than 35 milligrams; and "low sodium" is less that 140 milligrams. "No salt added" means no salt was added during processing of food; products could still have a high level of naturally occurring sodium.

USEFUL STAPLES

What are the indispensable ingredients of healthier eating? Your refrigerator, freezer or pantry shelves should provide fat-free, salt-free chicken and vegetable stocks; nonfat and sodium-reduced dairy products; salt free tomato preparations; lots of vegetables and fruits (fresh or canned without salt, or in fruit juices); a variety of grains and beans; and salt-free seasonings.

Several years ago most of these foods had to be prepared at home; now it is possible to find commercially processed versions of all these necessities in most supermarkets. If your grocer doesn't carry the products you need, speak to the store manager or write to the food manufacturers listed at the end of this chapter to find the suppliers nearest to your home.

More ambitious cooks still enjoy making their own healthy, basic foods. Homemade foods cost less than the commercially prepared varieties, and you can be certain of the ingredients. Set aside one evening or part of the day to prepare stocks, beans and tomato sauce. Plan ahead, so that the beans soak overnight and the freezer containers are washed and ready. in just a few hours, you will have filled your freezer and earned a grand feeling of satisfaction. Plus the foods you make yourself have an extra special seasoning that nothing brought home from the supermarket can match!

UNSALTED, DEFATTED CHICKEN STOCK

Use either a whole chicken cut into pieces or the wings, backs and skin you've collected and frozen, waiting for the day you make stock.

3–4 lb. chicken parts
6 black peppercorns
cold water
2 carrots, scrubbed and sliced
1 celery rib, sliced (include leaves)
2 cloves garlic, minced

1 medium onion, peeled and halved, or 1–2
  green onions, chopped
1 bay leaf
2–3 sprigs parsley
1 tbs. chopped fresh herbs of your choice:
  thyme, dill, oregano, or 1 tsp. dried

Place chicken and peppercorns in a large stock pot. Add cold water to cover and bring to a boil over high heat. Reduce heat and simmer, uncovered, for half an hour. Add vegetables and seasonings. Cover and simmer for two hours. Strain and discard vegetables and chicken (or save for other uses). Chill stock several hours or overnight. Fat will rise to the surface and solidify; lift and discard it. Stock can now be used or frozen for the future. (To have small amounts of stock instantly available, freeze in ice cube trays and store in an airtight container.)

per cup 12 calories, 0.1 g protein, 29 g carb., 0.5 g fat, 2 mg cholesterol, 5 mg sodium

VEGETABLE STOCKS

An easy method: Get into the habit of saving the cooking water from every vegetable you prepare. Pour this liquid into a container in your freezer. Use these blended vegetable juices as a stock supply that never runs dry.

Another method: Collect scrubbed vegetable tops and peelings as you cook. Include carrot or parsnip tops, broccoli or mushroom stems, potato peelings, tomato or celery trimmings, etc. (These tidbits can also be saved in the freezer.) When you are ready, combine all the pieces in a saucepan, cover with water and bring to a boil. Reduce heat and simmer, uncovered, for 30 to 45 minutes. Strain and store as for *Chicken Stock* on page 8.

Easiest method: Cover 1 or 2 tablespoonfuls of dried vegetable bits (found on the grocer's spice shelves) with boiling water. Let steep for a few minutes, and then strain to use.

TOMATO PRODUCTS

Almost all supermarkets now carry tomato products with reduced sodium or no salt added; however, if you have a bumper crop in your garden or if you just feel in the mood, these homemade tomato sauces can be made in large quantities and they freeze well.

EASY TOMATO SAUCE

Makes 3¹/₂ cups

1 medium onion, chopped
¹/₂ cup defatted chicken or vegetable stock
3 cups coarsely chopped fresh, ripe
   tomatoes
1 tsp. frozen apple juice concentrate
1 tsp. minced fresh thyme, or ¹/₂ tsp. dried

1 tsp. minced fresh oregano, or ¹/₂ tsp. dried
1 tsp. minced fresh basil, or ¹/₂ tsp. dried
1 clove garlic, minced or mashed
1 clove garlic, minced or mashed
freshly ground black pepper

In a medium saucepan, cook onions in stock until soft. Add remaining ingredients. Bring to a boil, cover and simmer for 30 to 45 minutes.

per ¹/₂ *cup* 27 calories, 1 g protein, 8 g carb., 0.3 g fat, 0 mg cholesterol, 8 mg sodium

ALL-PURPOSE TOMATO SAUCE

Makes 3 cups

1 cup unsalted, defatted chicken or vegetable stock
1 large onion, chopped
1–2 cloves garlic, minced or mashed
1 rib celery, chopped
1 small carrot, grated
1/2 cup unsalted tomato paste
3 cups coarsely chopped tomatoes
1 bay leaf
4–5 tbs. fresh basil, minced or 1 tsp. dried
2–3 sprigs fresh parsley, minced, or 1 tsp. dried
freshly ground black pepper

In a large saucepan, heat 1/2 cup stock; cook onion, garlic, celery and carrot until tender. Add remaining stock and all other ingredients. Stir well, bring to a boil, reduce heat and simmer, covered, 30 to 45 minutes. Remove bay leaf. For smooth sauce, process in blender or food processor for 30 to 45 seconds.

per 1/2 cup 55 calories, 2.1 g protein, 16.8 g carb., 0.5 g fat, o mg cholesterol, 33 mg sodium

STEWED TOMATOES

Some manufacturers now make special versions of stewed tomatoes—Creole, Italian, Mexican—most with added salt. Create your own salt-free products! Season the basic mix with cayenne pepper for Creole; with basil, oregano and extra garlic for Italian; with oregano and cinnamon for Greek; or with hot or mild chiles for Mexican.

1/4 cup unsalted, defatted chicken stock
1/4 green bell pepper, chopped
2–3 ribs celery, chopped
1 medium onion, chopped
2 1/2–3 cups chopped tomatoes
1–2 tsp. seasonings of your choice (see above)
freshly ground black pepper

In a large saucepan, heat stock to simmering. Add green pepper, celery and onions, and cook until soft. Add remaining ingredients. Bring to a boil and simmer 10 minutes.

per serving *55 calories, 2 g protein, 14.3 g carb., 0.5 g fat, 0 mg cholesterol, 40 mg sodium*

SALSA

An all-purpose Mexican-style sauce can add a piquant flavor to many dishes. Visit a Mexican market to find peppers that vary in flavor and hotness—Anaheim, serrano, ancho. for larger quantities, multiply amounts and freeze. Canned chiles should be drained and rinsed to remove brine.

2 cups finely chopped tomatoes
2–3 green onions, finely chopped
2–3 sprigs fresh parsley, finely chopped
2–3 cloves garlic, minced or mashed

1 fresh chile pepper, seeded and finely
   chopped, or 1 can (3$1/2$ oz.) hot chile
   peppers, seeded and chopped
$1/2$ tsp. dried oregano

Combine all ingredients and chill for several hours.

NOTE: The hottest parts of fresh chiles are the seeds, inner membranes and juices. Cut them carefully, and wash your hands well with soap and water afterwards. Avoid touching your hands to your face and especially your eyes while cutting peppers.

---

per 1/4 cup *16 calories, 0.7 g protein, 3.5 g carbo, 0.2 g fat, o mg cholesterol, 6.23 mg sodium*

BASIC WHITE SAUCE OR SOUP

For all your old favorites, like clam sauce, or curried shrimp—a butterless, fat-free, salt-free white sauce. To make cream soup, double the amount of stock called for, or add an equivalent amount of non-fat (skim) milk.

$1/2$ cup nonfat instant dry milk
1 tbs. all-purpose flour
1 tbs. cornstarch or arrowroot

freshly ground white pepper to taste
1 cup unsalted, defatted chicken or
    vegetable stock

In a small saucepan, combine dry milk, flour, cornstarch and pepper. Add stock slowly, stirring until smooth. Cook over low heat, stirring constantly, until sauce thickens.

per $1/4$ cup   *48 calories, 15 g carb., 0.2 g fat, 2 mg cholesterol, 48 mg sodium*

VARIATIONS

Add 1 cup sliced mushrooms that have been cooked in $1/4$ cup of stock

Add 2 to 3 tbs. chopped fresh chives

Add freshly grated nutmeg (great over steamed vegetables)

SUBSTITUTE CREAM

This "cream" can be used in any fruit or vegetable dish and in fish, chicken or pasta recipes that use heavy cream. It holds up when cooked and in gelatin dishes. Flavored with fruit concentrates or puréed fruit, it makes delicious toppings for plain cakes and fruit.

2 cups nonfat or low-fat, low-sodium ricotta cheese
1/2 cup nonfat, plain yogurt

Combine cheese and yogurt in food processor and purée until very smooth. The mixture should not be grainy. Pour the "cream" into a bowl, cover and let stand at room temperature for 4 to 6 hours. Refrigerate in a covered bowl. Keeps for 7 to 10 days.

*per **1/4 cup** 62 calories, 6 g protein, 2 g carb., 2 g fat, 0 mg cholesterol, 22 mg sodium*

ADAPTING FAVORITE RECIPES

Just a few changes in technique will make your old favorites conform to new standards. Here we offer guidelines; the recipes will give specifics.

HOW TO BROWN WITHOUT FAT, SAUTE WITHOUT SHORTENING

Preheat the broiler. Place meat or chicken one rack in the broiler pan. Brown on all sides.

Use a nonstick pan, wok or heavy skillet that has been coated with nonstick spray. (Always spray before heating.) Heat the pan before adding meat, vegetables or grains.

Place 1 or 2 tablespoonsful of chicken or vegetable stock in a skillet. Heat until simmering. Add ingredients, and stir frequently to prevent burning. Add more stock as needed to prevent sticking, but not so much that ingredients are boiled.

HOW TO MARINATE WITHOUT OIL

So many marinades use oil to distribute seasonings through a food. Substitute one of the liquids that follow for the oil in your favorite marinade, and add your familiar seasonings.

Plain nonfat yogurt

Juices such as lemon, orange or tomato

Wine or vinegar

Tomato-based products

Mustards, either plain or flavored

Or use a combination of the ingredients above: yogurt with mustard or juice, vinegar with mustard; tomato sauce with yogurt.

HOW TO ADD EGGS WITHOUT CHOLESTEROL, OR CREAM WITHOUT FAT

Substitute 2 egg whites for 1 whole egg.

Use an egg substitute wherever whole eggs are called for.

Where the recipe separates eggs, use the whites but discard the yolks; use 2 tbs. egg substitute for each yolk.

Buy the new fat-free dairy products, cream cheese, sour cream alternative (not the nondairy kind!), but be aware that many of these products are high in sodium.

Use low-fat, low sodium ricotta cheese for cool, white creaminess.

Use our homemade *Yogurt "Cheese"*, page 26, or *Substitute Cream,* page 15.

A FEW OF OUR FAVORITE THINGS

Many manufacturers these days offer a variety of foods low in fat, salt and sugar; however, some products are still hard to find outside of natural food stores. The list that follows will help you locate these foods in your area or via mail order or the internet. Several internet stores now carry an excellent selection of health foods. We include a few suggestions.

CANNED KIDNEY, PINTO OR GARBANZO BEANS, very low sodium

AMERICAN PRAIRIE Brand

Mercantile Food Company

P. O. Box SS

Philmont, NY 12565-0826

(518) 672-0190, (518) 672-0198 fax

Email: Merfood@aol.com

EDEN FOODS Brand

701 Tecumseh Road

Clinton, Michigan 49236

www.edenfoods.com

SALSA, no salt added

Healthy Heart Market

P. O. Box 459

Rogers, Minnesota 55374

1-888-685-5988

www.healthyheartmarket.com

SPAGHETTI SAUCE, no salt added

ENRICOS'S SPAGHETTI SAUCE

Ventre Packing Co.

Syracuse, NY 13204

CORN CHIPS, **baked-not-fried, no salt added**

GUILTLESS GOURMET
GMB Enterprises, Inc.
340 Marin Blvd.
Jersey City, New Jersey 07302
www.guiltlessgourmet.com

BEARITOS CHIPS
Little Bear/Bearitos Consumer Relations
The Hain Celestial Group, Inc.
4600 Sleepytime Dr.
Boulder, CO 80301
www.Littlebearfoods.com

NONFAT SOUR CREAM

KNUDSEN FREE
Knudsen Division of Kraft General Foods
Kraft Consumer Information
800-323-0768

DRIED TOMATO PRODUCTS & ORGANIC FRUITS

SONOMA PRODUCTS
Timber Crest Farms
4791 Dry Creek Road
Healdsburg,CA 95448
888-374-9325

ALL-FRUIT SWEETENERS

WAX ORCHARDS FRUIT SWEET
Wax Orchards Inc
22744 Wax Orchards Road SW
Vashon Island, WA 98070
800-634-6132

SOME INTERNET HEALTH FOOD STORES

http://www.shopnatural.com/
http://www.followyourheart.com/
http://www.mothernature.com/

APPETIZERS AND SNACKS

21 Creamy Tofu Dip
22 Spicy Tofu Spread
23 White Bean Spread
24 Spicy Bean Dip
25 Eggplant Dip
26 Yogurt "Cheese"
27 Green Garden Yogurt Cheese Dip
28 Herbed Yogurt Cheese Dip

29 Layered Cheese Torta
30 Onion-Dill Dip
31 Apple Curry Dip
32 Stuffed Mussels
33 Peach Chutney
34 Cheese Ball
35 Crunchy Cabbage Slaw

No one wants to give up snacks or to stop entertaining simply because of a new consciousness about healthy eating. Subtle changes can make your familiar appetizers and dips conform to new standards. What goes with dips besides chips? Lots of things. Toasted triangles of pita bread or tortillas, or fat-free crackers. In addition to the usual celery and carrots, try less widely known vegetables such as crisp slices of kohlrabi or turnip, briefly cooked asparagus, whole green beans or florets of broccoli or cauliflower. Instead of candy, snack on fruits dried without sugar or hot-air popped corn sprinkled with your favorite salt-free seasoning blend.

CREAMY TOFU DIP

Makes 1 cup

For centuries, Chinese and Japanese cooks have used tofu, a high quality protein made from soybeans. Now most Americans can find tofu in their supermarkets, in a variety of forms—soft, firm, water-packed or dry. Before using, water-packed tofu should be sliced and pressed between paper towels to remove excess moisture.

1 cup tofu, mashed
1 clove garlic, minced or mashed
1/2 cup finely chopped green onions
1 tbs. finely chopped fresh parsley
1/2 cup plain nonfat yogurt
1 tsp. unsalted, Dijon-style mustard
freshly ground pepper

Combine all ingredients in a blender or food processor, and process until thoroughly blended. Chill several hours or overnight. Serve with pita bread triangles, unsalted fat-free crackers, or sliced raw vegetables.

per tablespoon *17 calories, 1.7 g protein, 1.2 g carb., 0.8 g fat, 0 mg cholesterol, 11 mg sodium*

SPICY TOFU SPREAD

Makes 1 cup

Although some supermarkets display tofu in the produce section, it should be kept under refrigeration like dairy products. Once opened, tofu should be stored in water in the refrigerator.

8 oz. tofu
1 tbs. nonfat or reduced fat mayonnaise
2 cloves garlic, minced or mashed
2 green onions, finely chopped
4–6 sprigs parsley, finely chopped
1/4 cup unsalted salsa

Pour water off tofu and drain on paper towels. Combine all ingredients in the bowl of a blender or food processor and process until smooth. Place mixture in a small bowl; cover and refrigerate for several hours. Serve with pita bread and/or raw vegetables.

per tablespoon *16 calories, 1.2 g protein, 0.9 g carb., 1 g fat, 0 mg cholesterol, 10 mg sodium*

WHITE BEAN SPREAD

Makes 1 cup

Substitute this spread for the cream cheese in your old veggie sandwich recipes, or serve it with sliced vegetables for an appetizer.

1 cup cooked white beans, well drained
1–2 cloves garlic, minced or mashed
2 tbs. lemon juice
2 tbs. finely chopped fresh parsley

Combine all ingredients in a blender or food processor and process until thoroughly blended. Chill several hours or overnight. Can be frozen; thaw in the refrigerator.

---
per tablespoon *11 calories, 0.7 g protein, 2 g carb., 0 g fat, 0 mg cholesterol, 0 mg sodium*

SPICY BEAN DIP

In winter, present the dip warmed in a chafing dish or over a candle-warmer, with a basket of toasted blue and yellow unsalted baked corn tortilla chips.

2 cups cooked pinto or kidney beans, well drained
1–2 cloves garlic, minced or mashed
1 tsp. unsalted Dijon-style mustard
2 tbs. canned diced green chiles (more for a spicier dip)
2 tsp. cider vinegar
2–3 drops Tabasco Sauce or to taste
2 tbs. grated nonfat cheddar cheese
1/4 cup thinly sliced green onions, for garnish

In a blender or food processor, combine all the ingredients except Tabasco and green onions. Process until smooth. If mixture seems too thick, add bean cooking liquid or stock. Add Tabasco carefully, drop by drop. Cover and chill overnight, to allow flavors to blend. Serve at room temperature or warmed, topped with green onions.

per tablespoon 16 calories, 1 g protein, 2.9 g carb., 0 g fat, 0 mg cholesterol, 10 mg sodium

EGGPLANT DIP

To peel or not to peel. That's up to you. Some cooks like the added fiber of the cooked peel; others prefer to discard the skin.

$^1/_4$ cup unsalted, defatted chicken or
   vegetable stock
1 eggplant, about 1$^1/_2$ lb., diced
1 cup unsalted tomato sauce
$^1/_2$ cup chopped green pepper
2 cloves garlic, minced or mashed

$^1/_2$ tsp. ground cumin
$^1/_4$ tsp. cayenne pepper
$^1/_4$ cup red wine or cider vinegar
$^1/_4$ cup finely chopped fresh cilantro, or 1
   tbs. dried
pita bread, cut into triangles

In a large skillet over medium heat, combine stock, eggplant, tomato sauce, green pepper, garlic, cumin, cayenne and vinegar. Cover and simmer 20 to 25 minutes. Uncover and cook over high heat, stirring, until most of the liquid has evaporated. Transfer mixture to a bowl, cover and chill at least 2 hours or as long as overnight. Just before serving, stir in cilantro, reserving 1 tbs. to sprinkle on top. Serve with pita bread triangles.

per tablespoon 9 calories, 0.4 g protein, 2 g carb., 0 g fat, 0 mg cholesterol, 3 mg sodium

YOGURT "CHEESE"

Makes 1³/₄ cups

Now that we find nonfat cream cheese on the dairy shelf, there is no need to make a substitute; still, this "cheese" has a tangy quality of its own, and it's lower in sodium than the nonfat product. Besides, it's fun to prepare.

Line a 4-cup strainer or colander with several thicknesses of dampened cheesecloth and place it over a bowl. Turn 4 cups of plain nonfat yogurt into the cheesecloth-lined strainer. (Read the label to be sure the yogurt does not contain gelatin.) Pull the ends of the cloth over the yogurt to cover it, and lay a weight on top to press it down. (A saucer with a package of dry beans on top makes a good weight.) Refrigerate the whole arrangement, and let the yogurt drip for 8 to 10 hours or overnight. Remove the "cheese" from the cloth and discard the whey that dripped into the bowl.

An alternate method: After the yogurt has been turned into the colander, gather two opposite corners of cheese cloth, cross them and tie them; do the same for the other two corners. Take up the ends of cheesecloth, tie them into a strong knot, and suspend the bundle of wrapped yogurt from the kitchen faucet overnight. The whey will drip into the sink, and you will have fresh cheese in the morning.

*per **1/4 cup** 47 calories, 6 g protein, 5.5 g carb., 0 g fat, 1 mg cholesterol, 53 mg sodium*

GREEN GARDEN YOGURT CHEESE DIP

Makes 1³/₄ cups

Besides serving as a dip for crackers or vegetables, this tempting spread may be used as a stuffing for cherry tomatoes. Nonfat cream cheese may be used in place of the yogurt cheese.

1 cup *Yogurt "Cheese"*, page 26, or nonfat cream cheese
¹/₂ cup finely chopped spinach leaves, washed and dried
¹/₄ cup finely chopped fresh parsley
1 green onion, finely chopped
1 tsp. unsalted Dijon-style mustard
1 tsp. dried oregano
1 tbs. finely chopped dried tomatoes

Combine all ingredients in bowl of blender or food processor. Process 30 seconds or until mixture is smooth and creamy. Store covered in the refrigerator.

per ¹/₄ cup 32 calories, 3.8 g protein, 4.1 g carb., 0 g fat, 1 mg cholesterol, 45 mg sodium

HERBED YOGURT CHEESE DIP

Makes 2 cups

A delicious, low-fat substitute for popular Boursin cheese.

1 cup peeled, grated cucumber
1 cup *Yogurt "Cheese"*, page 26
1/4 cup fresh lemon juice
1 tbs. minced fresh dill weed or 1 tsp. dried
2 cloves garlic, minced or mashed
1–2 drops Tabasco Sauce
freshly ground pepper to taste

Press cucumber between 2 paper towels to remove excess moisture. In a small bowl, combine cucumber and remaining ingredients. Chill 2 to 3 hours before serving to allow flavors to blend.

*per **1/4 cup** 29 calories, 3.2 g protein, 4.3 g carb., 0 g fat, 1 mg cholesterol, 27 mg sodium*

LAYERED CHEESE TORTA

The amounts and kinds of vegetables are approximate. Mix and match to your taste.

4 cups *Yogurt "Cheese"*, page 26
2–3 cloves garlic, minced or mashed
1 tsp. dry mustard
1 medium tomato, chopped
1 tbs. chopped dried tomatoes

2 green onions, finely chopped
2–3 sprigs parsley, finely chopped
1/2 red or yellow pepper, chopped
1/2 cup chopped frozen artichoke hearts
4 black olives, finely chopped

Combine yogurt cheese, garlic and mustard, and beat until smooth. Set aside. Combine remaining ingredients. Line an 8-inch round baking pan with wax paper. Cover paper with cheese mixture. Chill. When mixture is hard, turn out on serving platter and top with vegetables. Cover with plastic wrap and refrigerate until serving.

Or, line a small flower pot or other mold with damp cheesecloth. Fill the mold with alternate layers of cheese and vegetables, beginning and ending with cheese. Fold the cheesecloth over and chill for at least 1 hour, or until cheese feels firm. Fold back the cheesecloth and invert the mold on a serving dish. Gently remove the mold and then the cheesecloth. Cover with plastic wrap and refrigerate until serving.

per serving *109 calories, 12.7 g protein, 14 g carb., 0.4 g fat, 2 mg cholesterol, 133 mg sodium*

ONION-DILL DIP

This mixture of ricotta cheese, onion and dill for raw vegetables also goes well with cooked ones. Just heat in a microwave and the dip turns into a sauce.

$1/4$ cup nonfat or low-fat, low sodium ricotta cheese
1 tbs. nonfat or reduced fat mayonnaise
1 cup plain nonfat yogurt
2 tbs. unsalted Dijon-style mustard
1 tbs. dried onion flakes
2 tsp. dried dill weed

Combine all ingredients in blender or food processor. Process 30 seconds or until mixture is smooth and creamy. Store covered in the refrigerator. Serve with raw vegetables or fat-free crackers.

per tablespoon *18 calories, 1.4 g protein, 1.8 g carb., 0.6 g fat, 2 mg cholesterol, 45 mg sodium*

APPLE CURRY DIP

Makes 1 cup

Sitting on a tuffet, eating it with curds, little Miss Muffet was the first to popularize whey, the main ingredient in ricotta cheese.

1 cup nonfat or low-fat, low sodium ricotta cheese
1 cup unsweetened applesauce
2 tsp. curry powder
1/2 tsp. cinnamon
1/2 tsp. freshly grated nutmeg

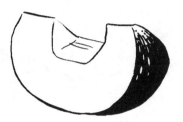

Combine all ingredients in blender or food processor. Process 30 seconds or until mixture is smooth and creamy. Store covered in the refrigerator. Serve with fresh apple slices, grapes, or sliced oranges.

per tablespoon *29 calories, 1.8 g protein, 2.8 g carb., 1.3 g fat, 5 mg cholesterol, 20 mg sodium*

STUFFED MUSSELS

Stuff mussel shells ahead of time if you like. Keep them in the refrigerator until time to heat.

1 cup water
1/4 cup dry white wine or vermouth
2–3 black peppercorns
2–3 slices lemon
2 lb. mussels, cleaned and scrubbed, "beards" removed
3–4 green onions, finely chopped

1 1/2 tsp. grated lemon peel (zest)
4–6 sprigs fresh parsley, finely chopped
1 cup crumbs made from fat-free, unsalted crackers or bread
1/8 tsp. crushed red chile pepper
2 egg whites, lightly beaten
2 tbs. grated nonfat cheese

Preheat oven to 350°. Combine water, wine, peppercorns, and lemon slices in a large pan. Bring to a boil; add mussels, cover and steam over high heat for about 6 to 8 minutes or until mussels open. Discard any that do not open. Remove mussels from shells; reserve broth and shells. Chop mussels. Heat 2 tablespoons reserved broth in a nonstick skillet; add onions and cook until soft, but not brown. Add chopped mussels; stir in remaining ingredients except cheese. Place about 1 tablespoon of mussel mixture on each shell; sprinkle with cheese. Place shells on baking sheet and bake for 10 minutes. Serve warm.

per serving 213 calories, 21.8 g protein, 19 g carb., 4.2 g fat, 43 mg cholesterol, 485 mg sodium

PEACH CHUTNEY

Makes 3$\frac{1}{2}$ cups

Commercial chutneys are often loaded with sugar. This version uses orange juice and raisins as sweeteners. Try it mixed with nonfat cream cheese or yogurt cheese. This may be frozen.

1 cup orange juice
$\frac{1}{4}$ cup rice vinegar
2 tbs. lemon juice
1 cup golden seedless raisins
1 small red onion, chopped
1 inch stick cinnamon

1 tbs. chopped ginger root
$\frac{1}{4}$ tsp. crushed red pepper flakes
1 tsp. freshly grated nutmeg
4 large peaches, coarsely chopped,or
   substitute nectarines or pears
2 tbs. slivered almonds

In a large saucepan, combine juice, vinegar, lemon juice, raisins, onions, cinnamon, ginger and crushed red pepper. Bring to a boil; reduce heat and simmer covered for 5 minutes. Add peaches and simmer uncovered for 30 to 40 minutes, stirring occasionally. The mixture will thicken so watch carefully the last 15 minutes. Add almonds to pan and simmer for 10 minutes. Pour into glass jars and store in refrigerator for up to 2 weeks.

per tablespoon *16 calories, 0.2 g protein, 3.8 g carb., 0.2 g fat, 0 mg cholesterol, 1 mg sodium*

CHEESE BALL

Nonfat cheeses now make it possible to enjoy this old party favorite. If using yogurt cheese, add 1/4 cup finely minced onion.

2 cups nonfat cream cheese or *Yogurt "Cheese"*, page 26
1 tbs. Worcestershire sauce
2 cloves garlic, minced or mashed
1 cup grated nonfat cheddar cheese
1/2 cup finely chopped parsley

Combine cream cheese, Worcestershire sauce and garlic in a blender or food processor and process until smooth. Add cheddar cheese and mix well. Line a 2-cup small bowl with plastic wrap. Place cheese mixture in lined bowl and pull up plastic wrap to form a ball. When cheese is cold and firm, unwrap and roll the ball in chopped parsley. Place on a serving platter, cover and refrigerate.

per tablespoon *12 calories, 1.5 g protein, 1.5 g carb., 0 g fat, 0 mg cholesterol, 14 mg sodium*

CRUNCHY CABBAGE SLAW

We like the added fiber and color of the apple skins, but if you prefer you may peel them.

2 cups shredded green cabbage
2 cups shredded zucchini
2–3 green onions, thinly sliced, including tops
2 apples, cut, cored and shredded
1/4 cup nonfat yogurt
1/4 cup reduced calorie mayonnaise
1 tbs. cider vinegar
1 tbs. sugar
1 tsp. poppy seeds
freshly ground black pepper

Combine vegetables and apples in a large bowl. In a small bowl, stir together yogurt, mayonnaise, vinegar, sugar and seeds. Toss with vegetables and apples. Season with freshly ground black pepper. Cover and chill for several hours.

per serving *120 calories, 2 g protein, 10.2 g carb., 7.8 g fat, 5 mg cholesterol, 18 mg sodium*

BREAKFAST

37	Breakfast Drinks	*43*	Backpackers' Cereal
37	Fruit Shake	*44*	Low-Fat Cheese Danish
37	Yogurt Shake	*45*	Spreads for Toast
38	Tomato-Yogurt Shake	*45*	Dried Fruit Spread
38	Tropical Refresher	*45*	Frozen Fruit "Jam"
39	Orange Milk Shakes	*46*	Nonfat French Toast
40	Fat-Free, Sugarless Granola	*47*	Pancakes
41	Apple and Oats Cereal	*48*	Basic Omelet or Scrambled Eggs
42	Fruit and Grain Cereal	*50*	Bran and Fruit Mini-Muffins

Although breakfast is rightly called the "most important meal of the day", many traditional breakfast foods — from doughnuts and sweet rolls to bacon or ham, eggs cooked in butter, pancakes with butter and syrup — rank high on the list of foods to avoid.

Take heart. Old habits can be changed where there is the will, a little imagination and some planning. A healthy breakfast doesn't have to consist of traditional breakfast foods. And careful reading of labels will identify those cereals that are high in fiber but low in sugar and fat, and spreads for bread that are all fruit, with no sugar added.

BREAKFAST DRINKS

For those who don't like a real breakfast or have no time for it, here is a drink-and-run alternative. Basic directions: place all the ingredients in the blender (cube fruit and remove seeds first). Blend for 30 to 45 seconds. For an even quicker breakfast, load the blender container at night and refrigerate. In the morning, process and drink.

FRUIT SHAKE   Servings: 2

1 cup nonfat milk
2 tbs. instant nonfat dry milk
2 ripe bananas, pears or peaches

1/4 tsp. cinnamon
1 tbs. apple juice concentrate

per serving 177 calories, 7 g protein, 38.5 g carb., 0.8 g fat, 3 mg cholesterol, 90 mg sodium

YOGURT SHAKE   Servings: 1

1 cup plain nonfat yogurt
1/2 cup fresh or frozen fruit

1 tbs. fruit juice concentrate

per serving 192 calories, 13.7 g protein, 34.1 g carb., 0.5 g fat, 4 mg cholesterol, 177 mg sodium

TOMATO-YOGURT SHAKE   Servings: 2

1 cup plain nonfat yogurt

1 cup tomato or mixed vegetable juice, no salt added

1 tsp. lemon juice

1/4 tsp. grated fresh ginger

per serving *85 calories, 7.5 g protein, 14 g carb., 0.3 g fat, 2 mg cholesterol, 99 mg sodium*

TROPICAL REFRESHER   Servings: 2

1 can (8 oz.) unsweetened, crushed pineapple

1 cup plain nonfat yogurt

1 banana

per serving *183 calories, 7.5 g protein, 40 g carb., 0.6 g fat, 2 mg cholesterol, 88 mg sodium*

ORANGE MILK SHAKES

Either of these shakes looks especially attractive in a tall glass garnished with a slice of orange cut halfway through and slipped over the edge. The second recipe is even lower in fat than the first, but just as flavorful.

ORANGE MILK SHAKE #1   Servings: 1

1 cup orange juice   1/4 cup instant nonfat dry milk
1/4 tsp. vanilla extract

---

per serving *172 calories, 7.7 g protein, 34.7 g carb., 0.6 g fat, 3 mg cholesterol, 96 mg sodium*

ORANGE MILK SHAKE #2   Servings: 2

1 cup water   1/2 cup frozen orange juice concentrate
1 cup nonfat milk   1/2 tsp. vanilla

---

per serving *156 calories, 6 g protein, 33 g carb., 0 g fat, 0 mg cholesterol, 65 mg sodium*

FAT-FREE, SUGARLESS GRANOLA

Makes 4 cups

For a complete breakfast, serve with raisins or sliced banana and nonfat yogurt or milk. Mix with unsweetened commercial cereals to make them more nutritious. Double or triple the recipe; it keeps well if it's refrigerated.

2 cups rolled oats
1 cup barley flakes
1 cup untoasted wheat germ
1/2 cup instant nonfat dry milk

1 tsp. cinnamon
1 tsp. nutmeg
1 tsp. vanilla or almond flavoring
3/4 cup unsweetened apple juice

Preheat oven to 350°. In a large bowl, stir dry ingredients together. Add vanilla to juice and mix with dry ingredients. Spread in a shallow nonstick baking pan or one that has been coated with nonstick spray. Bake for 15 minutes. Stir mix, lower heat to 225° and continue baking until cereal is dry. Stir occasionally to prevent sticking and allow even browning. Drying time is approximately 2 hours, depending on size of pan.

per cup *326 calories, 16.2 g protein, 56.6 g carb., 5.2 g fat, 2 mg cholesterol, 50 mg sodium*

APPLE AND OATS CEREAL

Servings: 2

A versatile breakfast that tastes good cold with nonfat milk, heated in the microwave or spread on toast and browned under the broiler.

1 medium apple, grated (or substitute 1 cup unsweetened applesauce)
3/4 cup apple juice
1 tbs. instant nonfat dry milk
1/2 cup rolled oats
2 tbs. raisins or dried currants
1/2 tsp. cinnamon or nutmeg

Mix apple with juice, or pour juice into a blender container, add apple and blend for 30 seconds. Stir in remaining ingredients and refrigerate.

per serving 197 calories, 4.5 g protein, 43 g carb., 1.7 g fat, 0 mg cholesterol, 16 mg sodium

FRUIT AND GRAIN CEREAL

Servings: 4

Do you like more fruit than cereal in your breakfast bowl? This one's for you.

3/4 cup unsweetened fruit juice of your choice
1 peach or nectarine, seeded and cubed
1 banana, sliced
1/2 cup oat bran (or other breakfast grain)
1/2 tsp. cinnamon or cardamom
1 cup plain nonfat yogurt

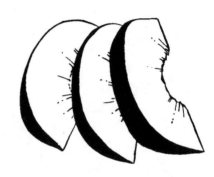

In a food processor or blender, blend juice and fruits until smooth. Combine oat bran and cinnamon in a small bowl. Pour fruit over and mix well. Cover and chill. Just before serving, stir in yogurt.

---

per serving *115 calories, 6 g protein, 26 g carb., 1 g fat, 1 mg cholesterol, 45 mg sodium*

BACKPACKERS' CEREAL

Servings: 4

A cereal for foot travelers or any other kind. More nutritious than packaged commercial varieties.

1 cup rolled oats
1 cup wheat flakes
1 cup barley flakes
1 cup instant nonfat dry milk
$1/2$ tsp. cinnamon
$1/2$ tsp. nutmeg
1 cup dried fruit (raisins, banana slices, chopped dates or apricots)

Preheat oven to 450°. Mix grains together and spread in a shallow pan. Toast in the oven until brown, about 5 to 7 minutes. (Watch closely and stir to prevent burning.) Remove from oven and cool. Stir in dry milk, seasoning and dried fruit. Store in an air-tight container. To serve, add hot water and mix.

per serving *398 calories, 16.8 g protein, 76.8 g carb., 4.1 g fat, 3 mg cholesterol, 102 mg sodium*

LOW-FAT CHEESE DANISH

Servings: 2

With a variety of fresh fruits and fruits canned in juices on hand, you can choose a different flavor for breakfast every morning of the week!

$1/2$ cup nonfat or 1% cottage cheese, or nonfat, low-sodium ricotta cheese
$1/4$ tsp. cinnamon, nutmeg or cardamom
$1/4$ tsp. vanilla
2 slices unsalted, whole wheat toast
4 slices pineapple canned in its own juice, or 1
   peach or nectarine, sliced

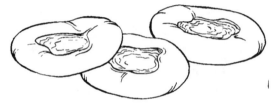

Mix cheese with seasonings. Divide and spread over toast. Lay 2 pineapple slices or half the peach slices on each slice of toast. Warm under broiler or in toaster oven until heated through.

per serving *192 calories, 11 g protein, 35 g carb., 2 g fat, 3 mg cholesterol, 260 mg sodium*

SPREADS FOR TOAST

Homemade spreads make wonderful gifts, even when the fruits are out of season.

DRIED FRUIT SPREAD

Makes 3¹/₂ cups

1 cup dried pears

1 cup dried peaches

1 cup dried apples

1 cup water or unsweetened apple juice

In a medium saucepan, combine fruits and liquid. Simmer until fruits are soft, about 10 minutes. Cool. Purée in a food processor or blender. Cover and store in the refrigerator.

per tablespoon 50 calories, 0.5 g protein, 13.1 g carb., 0.1 g fat, 0 mg cholesterol, 4 mg sodium

FROZEN FRUIT "JAM"

Makes 1¹/₂ cups

1¹/₂ cups unsweetened frozen fruit, sliced

1¹/₂ tbs. quick cooking tapioca

¹/₄ cup frozen fruit juice concentrate of choice

In a small saucepan, mix together fruit, juice concentrate and tapioca. Let sit for 5 minutes. Bring to a boil over medium heat, stirring often. Cool for 20 minutes. Cover and refrigerate.

per tablespoon 13 calories, 0 g protein, 3 g carb., 0 g fat, 0 mg cholesterol, 1 mg sodium

NONFAT FRENCH TOAST

If you tend to run out of time in the morning, prepare the egg-soaked bread the night before, refrigerate it and warm it in the microwave before cooking.

1 egg white, or reduced fat egg product equal to 1 egg
1/4 cup nonfat milk
1/2 tsp. vanilla
1/2 tsp. dried orange bits
2 slices unsalted, day-old bread
all-fruit spread of your choice

Preheat broiler or a nonstick pan. Beat egg white or egg product until frothy. Add milk and seasonings. Dip bread slices in mix and turn until all liquid is absorbed. Place on a rack under the broiler and brown each side about 3 minutes, or brown slices in a nonstick pan, turning as needed. Serve hot with all-fruit spread of your choice.

per serving w/out spread 189 cal., 10.4 g protein.,
31.5 g carb., 1.9 g fat, 3 mg cholesterol, 205 mg sodium

PANCAKES

You can substitute all-purpose flour for the flours called for here, but you'll lose some of the texture and flavor.

$1/2$ cup unbleached white flour
1 cup whole wheat flour
2 tsp. low-sodium baking powder
1 cup nonfat milk
2 egg whites, slightly beaten, or reduced-fat
  egg product equal to 2 eggs

$1/2$–1 cup fresh or frozen blueberries,
  optional
1 tbs. dried orange bits, optional
all-fruit spread of your choice

Preheat a nonstick griddle or one that has been coated with nonstick spray. Sift dry ingredients into a large bowl. Beat together milk and egg whites or egg product. Stir egg into dry ingredients until just moistened. Carefully stir in blueberries and orange bits. Drop batter by spoonfuls onto preheated griddle. Cook until bubbles appear; turn and cook other side. Serve hot with all-fruit spread of your choice.

per pancake w/out spread 76 cal., 3.8 g protein, 15 g carb., 0.3 g fat, 1 mg cholesterol, 82 mg sodium

BASIC OMELET OR SCRAMBLED EGGS

The ingredients are the same—the difference is in the cooking.

1/2 cup reduced-fat egg product, equal to 2 eggs
1/4 cup nonfat milk
salt-free seasoning blend of your choice

Coat an omelet pan or 8-inch skillet with nonstick spray. Heat over moderate flame. While pan is heating, beat egg product with milk and seasoning. When pan is hot, pour egg mix into pan; reduce heat to low.

For omelet: As egg begins to set, lift cooked edge and tilt pan so uncooked mixture runs underneath. Continue to lift and tilt until egg is set but still shiny. Remove pan from heat. With a spatula, loosen all the way around. Lay filling, if desired, across center. With spatula, fold one edge over filling. Tilt pan and roll omelet onto plate.

For scrambled eggs: As egg begins to set, lift edge and move cooked egg to the center of the pan, continuing until done to your liking.

---

per serving w/out filling *52 cal., 12 g protein, 3.8 g carb., .1 g fat, 1 mg chol., 191 mg sodium*

FILLINGS FOR OMELET

- Mushroom omelet: $1/2$ cup mushrooms cooked in $1/4$ cup stock
- Jelly omelet: 3 tbs. of your favorite spreadable fruit product
- Spanish omelet: 1 tbs. each diced onion, green bell pepper and tomato, seasoned with a pinch each of oregano and rosemary.

BRAN AND FRUIT MINI-MUFFINS

Makes 24 muffins

Vary the fruit in these fiber-rich muffins—sweet or tart cherries, crushed pineapple, banana. Just be certain that canned or frozen fruits are prepared without added sugar.

1 cup Nabisco 100% Bran cereal
1/2 cup nonfat (skim) milk
2 tbs. all-fruit sweetener
reduced-fat egg product equal to 1 egg

1/4 tsp. vanilla extract
1/2 cup all-purpose flour
1 tsp. baking powder
1/2 cup finely chopped fresh or frozen fruit

Preheat oven to 375°. Coat miniature muffin pan or cups with nonstick spray. In a small bowl, combine cereal, milk, sweetener, egg product and vanilla. Set aside for 5 minutes. In a larger bowl, combine flour and baking powder. Stir cereal mix into flour just until blended. Carefully stir in fruit. Spoon into prepared muffin cups. Bake 12 to 15 minutes, until toothpick inserted in center comes out clean. Remove to a rack to cool.

per muffin *22 calories, 1 g protein, 4.6 g carb., 0.3 g fat, 1 mg cholesterol, 26 mg sodium*

BEANS

52 Cooking Times for Beans
54 Mexican-Style Beans
55 Bean Pita Pizza
56 Garbanzo Beans With Spinach
57 Red Red Bean Salad

58 Baked Beans With a Bite
59 Italian-Style Pasta and Beans
60 Enchiladas
61 Lentils With Creamy Mint Sauce
62 Fruit-Flavored Sweet Beans

Beans, part of a man's diet since Biblical times, have now been recognized as a valuable source of fiber, protein, vitamins and minerals. To serve beans, one can either cook dry beans or purchase the canned variety. We offer instructions for cooking with both kinds and give beans a starring role for low-fat, low-sodium cooking.

TRADITIONAL COOKING METHOD FOR DRY BEANS

1. Rinse dry beans in cold water; pick out any foreign material.

2. Soak beans in cold water for at least 6 hours and discard soaking water.

3. Add fresh water to beans, approximately 2 to 3 cups of water to each cup of dry beans. Bring water to a boil, reduce heat, cover and simmer until beans are soft.

QUICK SOAK METHOD

1. Rinse beans in cold water; pick out any foreign material.

2. Place beans in a large pot. Cover with cold water. Bring to a boil and boil for 5 minutes. Remove from heat and cover for 1 hour.

3. Drain and proceed to cook as in traditional method.

NOTE: A 1 lb. package of dry beans equals 2 cups dry or 5 to 6 cups cooked beans.

PRESSURE COOKER AND CROCK POT

Follow directions that accompany appliance.

APPROXIMATE COOKING TIMES FOR BEANS

Pinto, garbanzo, kidney and black beans: 2 to $2^{1}/_{2}$ hours

Small white beans: 1 hour

Lentils (no soaking required): 30 to 45 minutes

CANNED BEANS

Look for canned beans that say "no salt added" or "very low sodium." If beans canned with salt are the only ones available, rinse with cold water and drain before using.

NOTE: A $15^{1}/_{2}$ oz. can, drained, equals $1^{2}/_{3}$ cups cooked beans.

BEAN FACTS

Do not add salt or baking soda to cooking water. These products reduce the amount of B-vitamins and toughen the cooked beans.

Onion, garlic, carrots, and/or celery may be added to cooking water for flavor.

Cooked beans will keep in the freezer up to 6 months.

Cooked beans will keep in the refrigerator 3 to 4 days.

The liquid that beans are cooked in makes excellent stock for soups.

Beans are high in soluble fiber, iron and B-vitamins.

Uncooked dry beans should be stored in an airtight glass or metal container in a cool, dry place. Do not refrigerate.

ADDITIONAL HINTS AND SUGGESTIONS

Mix and match varieties of beans; for example use a combination of black, red and white beans in salads.

Marinate cooked beans in the juice saved from the salt-free pickles; add to salads.

Add leftover cooked beans to vegetable salads, stews and soups.

MEXICAN-STYLE BEANS

Several food companies now offer canned, black beans with no added fat. The spicy mixture in this recipe makes for an easy supper when served over toasted English muffins.

2 cups cooked or reduced-sodium, canned black beans
1/2 cup frozen corn, thawed
1/4 cup unsalted salsa, (mild or hot)
1 cup grated, nonfat cheddar cheese
4 English muffins, split
1/2 cup chopped red bell pepper, salad sprouts or chopped green onions

In a medium saucepan, combine black beans, corn and salsa. Cook uncovered over medium heat for 10 minutes. Add cheese and simmer for 2 to 3 minutes or until cheese begins to melt. Toast English muffins. Place a portion of beans on each muffin and top with red bell pepper, sprouts or green onions.

per serving *318 calories, 20.4 g protein, 52.5 g carbo, 2.2 g fat, 5 mg cholesterol, 598 mg sodium*

BEAN PITA PIZZA

Toasted pita bread makes a quick crust for pizzas. Use the mini pitas and serve as an appetizer.

2 tbs. unsalted, defatted vegetable stock or nonstick spray
1 small onion, chopped
2–3 cloves garlic, minced or mashed
1 tsp. dry mustard
2 cups cooked or reduced-sodium, canned pinto beans

2 cups cooked or reduced-sodium canned black beans
1¹/₂ cups salsa, no salt added
1 tsp. dried basil leaves
1 tsp. dried oregano
4 large pita breads, split
1 cup grated, nonfat cheese

Preheat oven to 375°. Heat 2 tbs. stock in a nonstick skillet or lightly coat pan with a nonstick spray. Add onions and cook until wilted; add garlic and mustard and cook for 2 minutes. Add beans, salsa and seasoning and simmer uncovered for 10 minutes. Meanwhile, place split pita bread on a cookie sheet and toast in oven. Top each toasted round with bean-salsa mixture and 2 tbs. grated cheese. Return to oven for 2 to 3 minutes or until cheese melts.

per serving *480 calories, 29.4 g protein, 82.5 g carb., 4 g fat, 5 mg cholesterol, 626 mg sodium*

GARBANZO BEANS WITH SPINACH

Offer chutney, chopped jicama or green onions and salt-free pickles as condiments for this vegetarian curry dish.

2 tbs. unsalted, defatted vegetable stock or
    nonstick cooking spray
1 large onion, chopped
2 large tomatoes, chopped
2–3 cloves garlic, minced or mashed
1 tsp. grated fresh ginger
1 tsp. dry mustard

2 cups cooked or reduced-sodium, canned
    garbanzo beans
2 cups chopped fresh spinach
1 tbs. curry powder
1/4 tsp. crushed red pepper flakes
freshly ground pepper to taste

Heat 2 tbs. stock in a nonstick skillet or lightly coat pan with nonstick spray. Add onion and tomatoes and stir-fry 3 to 5 minutes. Add garlic, ginger and mustard; cook for 2 minutes. Add beans, spinach, curry powder and crushed red pepper. Cook uncovered over medium heat for 10 minutes. Season with black pepper. Serve warm.

per serving *171 calories, 9.1 g protein, 30.2 g carb., 2.5 g fat, 0 mg cholesterol, 35 mg sodium*

RED RED BEAN SALAD

Servings: 4

A combination of red beans, red potatoes and red onions served over fresh red lettuce and garnished with finely chopped red radishes makes for a spectacular salad. We suggest using reduced-calorie bottled Italian dressing, but there is now a variety of nonfat salad dressings available.

6 small red potatoes, cooked, about 4 oz. each
1 carrot, finely chopped
1/2 small red onion, finely chopped
1 cup cooked or reduced-sodium, canned red beans

2 ribs celery, chopped
4–6 sprigs fresh parsley, finely chopped
1/4 cup nonfat salad dressing
lettuce and radish as garnish

In a medium-size bowl combine potatoes, carrots, onion, beans, celery and parsley. Pour salad dressing over vegetables and toss to coat all ingredients. Cover and let marinate several hours before serving. Arrange red lettuce on serving platter, cover with salad and garnish with radishes.

per serving *266 calories, 8.5 g protein, 55.5 g carb., 2 g fat, 1 mg cholesterol, 158 mg sodium*

BAKED BEANS WITH A BITE

Green chiles and crushed red pepper flakes add spice and flavor to these quickly prepared baked beans. Add chili powder to taste and remember that all chiles vary in intensity from mild to hot. Choose accordingly.

2 tbs. unsalted, defatted chicken or
   vegetable stock or nonstick cooking spray
1 medium onion, chopped
2–3 cloves garlic, minced or mashed
2 cups cooked or reduced-sodium, canned
   pinto or kidney beans

1 can (3 1/2 oz.) diced green chiles
1/4 tsp. crushed red pepper flakes
1 to 2 tbs. chili powder
1 can (14 1/2 oz.) unsalted stewed tomatoes

Preheat oven to 350°. Heat 2 tbs. stock in a nonstick skillet or lightly coat pan with nonstick spray. Add onions and garlic and stir-fry until onions begin to brown. Combine beans, green chiles, crushed red pepper flakes, chili powder and stewed tomatoes in a 1-quart baking pan. When onions and garlic are cooked, add to bean mixture. Cover and bake for 1 hour.

per serving *163 calories, 9.7 g protein, 31 g carb., 1 g fat, 0 mg cholesterol, 36 mg sodium*

ITALIAN-STYLE PASTA AND BEANS

Servings: 4

Finely chopped, dried tomato bits are usually found in specialty grocery stores. They keep well in the refrigerator and are a tasty addition to low-sodium cooking.

2 tbs. unsalted, defatted vegetable stock or nonstick olive oil spray
1 small onion, chopped
2–3 cloves garlic, minced or mashed
2 cups chopped mushrooms
1/2 red bell pepper, chopped
1/2 tsp. dry mustard

1/2 tsp. paprika
1 tbs. finely chopped, dried tomato bits
2 cups cooked or reduced-sodium, canned black or red beans
1 cup salad macaroni or pasta of your choice

Heat 2 tbs. stock in a nonstick skillet or lightly coat pan with nonstick spray; add onion, garlic, mushrooms, red bell pepper, mustard and paprika. Stir-fry until vegetables are wilted, about 5 minutes. Add tomato bits and beans. Cook uncovered over low heat for 15 minutes. Bring a large pan of water to a boil, add pasta and cook according to package directions. Drain and add beans. Serve warm.

per serving *227 calories, 12 g protein, 44.5 g carb., 1 g fat, 0 mg cholesterol, 6 mg sodium*

ENCHILADAS

Corn tortillas are easier to roll if they are warm. Place in a 200° oven for a few minutes before adding the filling.

2 tbs. unsalted, defatted vegetable stock or
   nonstick cooking spray
1 small onion, chopped
2–3 cloves garlic, minced or mashed
2 medium tomatoes, chopped
1 tbs. finely chopped, dried tomato bits

1 cup unsalted salsa
1 cups *Baked Beans with a Bite*, page 58, or
   1 can (15 oz.) fat-free chili
12 corn tortillas
1 cup grated, nonfat cheddar cheese

Preheat oven to 350°. Heat 2 tbs. stock in a nonstick skillet or lightly coat pan with nonstick spray. Add onions and garlic and cook until onion is wilted; add tomatoes and tomato bits and cook uncovered over low heat for 10 minutes. Stir in salsa. Place about 2 tbs. of beans on each tortilla; roll jellyroll-style and place seam side down in 9-x-13-inch baking dish that has been coated with nonstick spray. Cover enchiladas with onion-tomato mixture. Bake for 25 minutes. Sprinkle cheese over all and continue baking until cheese melts.

per serving *358 calories, 19 g protein, 63.3 g carb., 5.1 g fat, 5 mg cholesterol, 342 mg sodium*

LENTILS WITH CREAMY MINT SAUCE

Servings: 4

The lentil has long pods like those of peas and beans. The seeds of the lentil are the part used as food. Lentil seeds can be described as shaped like a lens. The lens itself was named because it looked like a small lentil seed.

2 cups plus 2 tbs. unsalted, defatted
   vegetable stock or nonstick cooking spray
1 small onion, chopped
2 cloves garlic, minced or mashed
1 tsp. grated fresh ginger
1 cup lentils

1 tsp. turmeric
1 tsp. dry mustard
$1/2$ cup nonfat, plain yogurt
$1/4$ cup grated cucumber
1 radish, finely chopped, optional
1 tsp. dried mint

Lightly coat pan with nonstick spray or heat 2 tbs. stock ina nonstick skillet. Add onions, garlic and ginger; cook until onions are soft, about 5 minutes. Add lentils, turmeric, mustard and remaining stock. Bring mixture to a boil, reduce heat, cover and simmer for 40 minutes. In a small bowl combine yogurt, chopped cucumbers, radish and mint. Place cooked lentils one serving dish and top with yogurt spread.

per serving *82 calories, 6.5 g protein, 14 g carb., 0.3 g fat, 1 mg cholesterol, 24 mg sodium*

FRUIT-FLAVORED SWEET BEANS

Most of us are familiar with red, white or black beans, but different varieties are showing up on supermarket shelves. You might find cranberry beans, Christmas limas, yellow eyes or Jacob's cattle. They look like the old reliables and may be used in any bean recipe.

2 tbs. unsalted, defatted vegetable stock or nonstick olive oil spray
1 medium onion, finely chopped
3 cups cooked or reduced-sodium, canned white beans
1 tsp. minced fresh ginger
2 tsp. ground cinnamon
freshly grated nutmeg to taste

1/4 cup frozen orange juice concentrate
1 cup white wine or white grape juice
1 cup pitted prunes
1 cup dried apples
1 apple or pear, chopped
1 cup apple juice
1 tbs. rum or sherry, optional

Preheat oven to 350°. Heat 2 tbs. stock in a nonstick skillet or lightly coat pan with non-stick spray; add onion and stir-fry until golden. Combine remaining ingredients in a 2-quart baking pan; mix in cooked onions. Cover pan and bake for 2 hours. If mixture becomes dry, add more apple juice.

per serving *398 calories, 8.8 g protein, 89 g carb., 0 mg cholesterol, 21 mg sodium*

BEEF

64 Athenian Market Stew
65 Meat Sauce With Zucchini
66 Bulgur and Meat Stew
67 Pita Pies With Cucumber Sauce

68 No-Fry Tacos
70 Nonfat Fajitas
71 Sweet and Golden Stew
72 Hungarian Goulash

Red meat has had bad press in recent years, but if you use good judgment and follow a few simple rules, you can still eat hearty beef meals. Limit your total meat consumption to no more than 4 or 5 ounces per day, and serve red meat only 1 or 2 times a week. Choose cuts of beef that are low in fat, like flank or round steak, and avoid the high-fat cuts like chuck and sirloin. Trim all visible fat from meat before you cook it. Be aware that dredging meat in flour before cooking seals in more fat. Instead, you may brown meat in a nonstick pan, in broth or under the broiler. Drain all fat from cooked ground meat before adding other ingredients. Substitute ground turkey or chicken for beef in highly seasoned casseroles or pasta sauces.

ATHENIAN MARKET STEW

All stews taste better the second day. Make it in advance and chill it, and you also gain time to remove any fat that you missed in preparation.

2 lb. boneless very lean beef

1 can (6 oz.) tomato paste

1 cup dry white wine (or substitute unsalted, defatted chicken stock)

1 tsp. ground cumin

1/2 tsp. freshly ground pepper

1–2 cloves garlic, minced or mashed

1 tbs. minced fresh mint, or 1 tsp. dried

1 bay leaf

1 small cinnamon stick

2 large onions, peeled and sliced

1/4 cup raisins

Trim meat of fat and cut into cubes. Brown under the broiler, or in a large, nonstick saucepan or Dutch oven, or one coated with nonstick spray. Drain and discard all fat. Turn meat out onto folded paper towels to absorb any remaining fat. Preheat oven to 300°. In a large, oven-proof casserole or Dutch oven, combine meat with tomato paste, wine, cumin, pepper, garlic, mint, bay leaf and cinnamon. Cover stew and bake for 1 hour, or until meat is tender. Add onions and raisins and cook for 10 to 20 minutes. Discard bay leaf and cinnamon stick before serving.

per serving *236 calories, 27 g protein, 11 g carb., 7 g fat, 76 mg cholesterol, 73 mg sodium*

MEAT SAUCE WITH ZUCCHINI

Use these tricks—combining ground turkey with ground beef; draining the fat; using non-fat cheese—in all your favorite ethnic recipes.

1/4 lb. lean ground turkey
1/4 lb. very lean ground beef
1/2 cup unsalted, defatted chicken stock
1 medium onion, chopped
1–2 cloves garlic, minced or mashed
2 cups cubed zucchini
2 cups unsalted tomato sauce

1 tbs. minced fresh basil, or 1 tsp. dried
1/2 cup chopped fresh mint, or 2 tbs. dried
1/4 tsp. crushed red pepper flakes, optional
freshly ground pepper to taste
12 oz. uncooked, egg-free pasta
1/2 cup shredded, nonfat cheese

Heat a large, deep nonstick skillet or one coated with nonstick spray. Brown meats; drain and discard all fat. Turn meat out onto folded paper towels to absorb any remaining fat, and wipe the skillet. In the same skillet, heat stock. Add onion and garlic and cook until tender. Add zucchini, cover and simmer until tender, about 5 minutes. Add browned meat, tomato sauce and seasonings. Simmer over low heat for 10 minutes. Cook pasta according to directions on package. Serve meat sauce over pasta, sprinkled with shredded cheese.

per serving *323 calories, 25 g protein, 45 g carb., 7 g fat, 47 mg cholesterol, 175 mg sodium*

BULGUR AND MEAT STEW

Here's a simple but easy way to stretch a small amount of meat.

1/2 lb. very lean ground beef
1/2 cup unsalted, defatted chicken stock
3 cups chopped onions
4 cups water or stock
1/4 cup dried garbanzo beans, soaked
  overnight

1 1/2 cups bulgur wheat
1 tsp. garam masala*
plain nonfat yogurt
chopped fresh parsley

Heat a large, nonstick saucepan or Dutch oven, or one coated with nonstick spray. Brown meat; drain and discard all fat. Turn meat out onto folded paper towels to absorb any remaining fat, and wipe the pan. In the same pan, heat stock. Add onions and cook until tender. Add meat, water and beans. Cover and simmer until beans are tender, about 1 hour. Add bulgur wheat and garam masala, and continue cooking for 45 minutes. Check occasionally and add extra water if mixture is dry. Serve garnished with yogurt and parsley.

per serving 357 calories, 21.3 g protein, 56.6 g carb., 7.8 g fat, 33 mg cholesterol, 43 mg sodium

*Garam masala is a mixture of ground cardamom, cumin, coriander, cinnamon, cloves and black pepper. Available in stores which carry Indian foods and spices.

PITA PIES WITH CUCUMBER SAUCE

Servings: 2

Serve one whole pie for a quick snack, two for a light supper, or a piece of pie as an appetizer.

2 pita bread rounds
1/2 lb. very lean ground beef
1/4 cup salsa with no salt or reduced salt

1/4 cup chopped green onions
Cucumber Sauce, follows

Preheat oven to 400°. Cut pita bread around edges and split to make 4 circles. Lay them on a baking pan with rough side up. Mix ground beef with salsa and onions. Divide among 4 circles of bread, and spread to edges. Bake for 10 minutes, or until meat is cooked through. Top with Cucumber Sauce.

per pie w/out sauce *326 cal., 34.7 g protein, 35.3 g carb., 7.2 g fat, 99 mg chol.7, 325 mg sodium*

CUCUMBER SAUCE

Makes 1 3/4 cups

1 cup plain nonfat yogurt
1–2 cloves garlic, minced or mashed

1 tbs. minced fresh mint, or 1 tsp. dried
1/2 cucumber, finely chopped

Combine all ingredients. Chill.

per tablespoon *6 calories, 0.5 g protein, 1 g carb., 0 g fat, 0 mg cholesterol, 6 mg sodium*

NO-FRY TACOS

When you eat these delicious tacos you'll never miss what's missing!

1/2 lb. very lean ground beef
1/2 lb. ground turkey
1/4 cup chopped green onions
1 cup unsalted or reduced sodium tomato sauce
1 can (3–4 ozs.) diced green chiles
1/2 tsp. ground cumin
1–2 cloves garlic, minced or mashed
1–2 tsp. chili powder
12 corn tortillas
garnishes: shredded lettuce, shredded zucchini, chopped green onions, chopped
   mushrooms, chopped tomatoes, grated nonfat cheese

Heat a large nonstick skillet or one that has been coated with nonstick spay. Brown beef and turkey, breaking meat into fine pieces; drain and discard all fat. Turn meat out onto folded paper towels to absorb any remaining fat, and wipe skillet. In the same skillet, combine meat with all remaining ingredients except tortillas and garnishes. Simmer uncovered 15 to

20 minutes. While simmering mixture, wrap tortillas tightly in foil and warm in a 250° oven. Let your family roll their own combinations of meat and garnishes.

---

per serving w/out garnish *275 cal., 20.5 g protein, 31.5 g carb., 8.3 g fat, 45 mg cholesterol, 219 g sodium*

FOR CRISP SHELLS

Preheat oven to 375°. Have tortillas at room temperature to prevent cracking. Loosely fold a limp tortilla over 2 rods of the oven rack so that it hangs down in the shape of a finished shell. Heat 5 to 7 minutes.

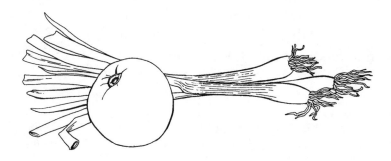

NONFAT FAJITAS

Bring the sizzling skillet to the table, so your family can enjoy the sound, aroma and color!

12 corn tortillas
1 lb. lean round or flank steak, cut into thin
   strips
1 large onion, sliced
1 red bell pepper, sliced into thin strips
1 green bell pepper, sliced into thin strips

1 tsp. chili powder
1/2 cup unsalted salsa
condiments: plain nonfat yogurt,
   shredded nonfat cheese, bean dip,
   chopped tomato, chopped green onion

Wrap tortillas tightly in foil and warm in a 250° oven. Heat a large, nonstick skillet, or one coated with nonstick spay. Brown meat; drain and discard all fat. Turn meat out onto folded paper towels to absorb any remaining fat and wipe pan. Return meat to pan; add onions and peppers. Cook over high heat, stirring and tossing, until vegetables are tender-crisp. Quickly stir in chili powder and salsa, and let your family roll their own meat and condiment combos in soft tortillas.

per serving without condiments 457 cal., 38 g protein,
99.3 g carb., 12.3 g fat, 59 mg cholesterol, 125 mg sodium

SWEET AND GOLDEN STEW

In this stew, the meat is just a condiment. Fruits and vegetables are the main ingredients.

1/2 lb. boneless, very lean beef, trimmed and cubed
1/4 cup whole wheat flour
3–4 sweet potatoes, scrubbed and cubed
1 cup chopped celery or kohlrabi

2–3 carrots, scrubbed and cut into rounds
1 cup unsweetened orange juice
1/2 tsp. cinnamon
3–4 tart apples, cored and quartered
1 cup pitted prunes

Brown meat under the broiler, or in a large, nonstick saucepan or Dutch oven, or one coated with nonstick spay. Drain and discard all fat. Turn meat out onto folded paper towels to absorb any remaining fat. Preheat oven to 300°. In a large, ovenproof casserole or Dutch oven, stir meat with flour. Add sweet potatoes, celery, carrots, orange juice and cinnamon. Cover and bake for 1 1/2 hours. Stir in apple and prunes, and bake 30 minutes longer, or until meat, vegetables and fruit are tender. If you prepare this stew in advance, do not add apples until you reheat to serve.

per serving 536 calories, 19.1 g protein, 113 g carb., 4.7 g fat, 38 mg cholesterol, 80 mg sodium

HUNGARIAN GOULASH

Curly noodles, which hold more sauce, work best with juicy goulash, but any noodle that doesn't contain eggs will work.

1 lb. lean cubed beef
1 large onion, sliced
1/2 cup dry red wine
2 tsp. sweet Hungarian paprika
1 tbs. tomato paste

1 cup sliced mushrooms
8 oz. uncooked noodles
1 cup plain nonfat yogurt or nonfat sour
  cream

Brown meat under the broiler, or in a large, nonstick saucepan or Dutch oven, or one coated with nonstick spray. Drain and discard all fat. Turn meat out onto folded paper towels to absorb any remaining fat. Return meat to pan. Add onion, red wine, paprika and tomato paste; simmer for 1 1/2 to 2 hours. About 20 minutes before serving, stir in mushrooms. Cook noodles according to package directions. Just before serving, remove meat from flame and stir in yogurt or nonfat sour cream. Serve goulash over cooked noodles.

per serving *252 calories, 30.8 g protein, 10.8 g carb., 7.3 g fat, 77 mg cholesterol, 106 mg sodium*

CHICKEN AND TURKEY

74	Chicken Strips With Basil
75	Chicken With Chutney
76	Braised Chicken With Sun-Dried Tomatoes
77	South-of-the-Border-Style Roast Chicken
78	Indian Chicken
79	Spicy Chicken With Dried Fruit
80	Cold Chicken With Mustard-Tomato Sauce
81	Crunchy Oven-Baked Chicken
82	Breast of Chicken With Orange Sauce
83	Chicken and Tortilla Casserole
84	Chicken and Potatoes
85	Chicken Simmered With Peaches
86	Turkey Breast With Sherry
87	Chicken Dijonnaise
88	Curried Chicken
89	Chicken With Mandarin Oranges

Chicken, if properly prepared, is low in fat and sodium. To keep it in the healthy category, the ingredients mixed, stirred and added to chicken recipes must also be low in fat and sodium. Breaded chicken parts that require frying are not part of low-fat cooking.

Chicken breasts without the skin are the best choice. A sharp knife is a must for separating the meat from the bones. To keep the breast from drying out, cook quickly over high heat when browning and then simmer in a flavorful broth or sauce. Adding bones to the broth adds flavor. We recommend removing the skin, which contains the most fat, before cooking.

CHICKEN STRIPS WITH BASIL

Servings: 4

Save this recipe for summertime when tomatoes are most flavorful and fresh basil is available. Dried basil leaves won't work here.

2 small tomatoes, chopped
2 cloves garlic, minced or mashed
1/2 cup finely chopped fresh basil
1/2 cup finely chopped fresh parsley
grated peel (zest) of 1 lemon
1 red or yellow bell pepper, chopped
2 tsp. unsalted Dijon-style mustard

1 tbs. herb vinegar
2 tbs. unsalted, defatted chicken
stock or nonstick olive oil spray
4 boneless, skinless chicken breast halves,
    cut into strips
freshly ground black pepper to taste
8 corn tortillas

Combine tomatoes, garlic, basil, parsley, lemon zest and bell pepper; mix in Dijon mustard and vinegar. Set mixture aside. Heat 2 tbs. stock in a nonstick skillet or lightly coat pan with nonstick spray. Add chicken strips and stir-fry until cooked through, about 5 minutes. Stir in tomato-basil mixture and cook about 3 minutes or until chicken is coated with basil mix. Season with pepper. Serve with warm, soft tortillas.

per serving 320 calories, 40.8 g protein, 34.3 g carb., 2 g fat, 97 mg cholesterol, 129 mg sodium

CHICKEN WITH CHUTNEY

Servings: 4

Historically chutneys were not sweetened—it was the colonial British who added sugar to the traditional Indian condiments. When purchasing commercial chutney, look for those whose first ingredient is fruit rather than sugar.

1/4 cup *Yogurt "Cheese"*, page 26, or nonfat cream cheese
2 tbs. *Peach Chutney*, page 33
1 tbs. unsalted, Dijon-style mustard
1 tsp. toasted sesame seeds
2 whole chicken breasts, split and skin removed
1/2 cup white wine
chopped chives for garnish

Preheat oven to 350°. Combine yogurt cheese, chutney, mustard and sesame seeds in a small bowl. Spread mixture on chicken breasts. Place chicken breasts in a shallow pan; pour wine into pan. Bake uncovered for about 30 minutes or until chicken is cooked through. Garnish with chopped chives.

per serving *202 calories, 36.8 g protein, 39.5 g carb., 1.7 g fat, 97 mg cholesterol, 86 mg sodium*

BRAISED CHICKEN WITH SUN-DRIED TOMATOES

Servings: 4

Plain sun-dried tomatoes that are not marinated in oil add great flavor to low-fat, low-sodium cooking. If you can only find the kind marinated in a jar, drain them on a paper towel.

1/2 cup unsalted, defatted chicken stock or
   nonstick cooking spray
2 whole chicken breasts, split and skin
   removed
1 medium onion, finely chopped
2–3 cloves garlic, minced or mashed

1/4 cup sun-dried tomatoes
1 cup sliced mushrooms
1/2 green or red bell pepper, finely chopped
1 tsp. dry mustard
1 tsp. dried basil leaves or oregano
1/4 cup dry white wine

Heat 2 tbs. stock in a nonstick skillet or lightly coat pan with nonstick spray. Brown chicken and set aside. In the same pan, cook onion, garlic, dried tomatoes and mushrooms until onion is golden; add pepper and stir-fry 3 to 4 minutes. Add seasonings, white wine and remaining chicken stock. Return chicken with its juices to pan. Cover pan and cook until chicken is done, 20 to 30 minutes.

per serving *202 calories, 36.8 g protein, 11.4 g carb., 1.7 g fat, 97 mg cholesterol, 92 mg sodium*

SOUTH-OF-THE-BORDER STYLE ROAST CHICKEN   Servings: 6

The roasting pan should be just large enough to hold the chicken; that way the juices from the chicken will be mixed with the spices. This is a holiday favorite.

2 cloves garlic, minced or mashed
1/2 tsp. cumin
1 tsp. ground coriander
1/8 tsp. crushed red pepper flakes
1 tsp. dry mustard
1 tbs. chili powder or to taste

freshly ground black pepper to taste
4 tbs. canned, diced green chiles or 1 fresh
   chile pepper, chopped
1 whole chicken, skin removed, about 3 lb.
3/4 cup plain nonfat yogurt
seeds from 1 pomegranate

Preheat oven to 350°. In a small bowl, combine garlic, cumin, coriander, pepper flakes, mustard, chili powder, black pepper and 2 tbs. of the green chiles; rub this mixture on chicken. Place chicken in small roasting pan with breast side up. Roast until chicken is cooked through, about 1 to 1 1/2 hours, basting occasionally with pan juices. To serve, slice chicken and place on platter. Mix yogurt with pomegranate and remaining 2 tbs. green chiles. Spoon over chicken.

per serving *305 calories, 50.5 g protein, 7.3 g carb., 7.1 g fat, 159 mg cholesterol, 263 mg sodium*

INDIAN CHICKEN

Garam masala, a pungent seasoning used in India, is a mixture of ground cardamom, cumin, coriander, cinnamon, cloves and black pepper. It is available in Indian markets.

2–3 cloves garlic, minced or mashed
2 tsp. grated fresh ginger
1$^1/_2$ tbs. curry powder or to taste
1 tsp. garam masala
2 tbs. lemon juice
2 tbs. whole wheat flour
2 green onions, finely chopped

2 tbs. finely chopped fresh parsley
1 cup plain, nonfat yogurt
2 whole chicken breasts, split and skin removed
1 small tomato, chopped
$^1/_4$ cup chopped water chestnuts

In a shallow baking pan large enough to hold chicken pieces in one layer, combine garlic, ginger, curry powder, garam masala, lemon juice, flour, onions, parsley, and nonfat yogurt. Add chicken pieces and coat with yogurt mixture. Cover pan and refrigerate for at least 6 hours or overnight. One hour before serving, preheat oven to 350°. Bake uncovered for about 50 minutes or until chicken is brown and cooked through. Garnish with chopped tomatoes and water chestnuts.

per serving 210 calories, 36.8 g protein, 9.7 g carb., 2 g fat, 83 mg cholesterol, 139 mg sodium

SPICY CHICKEN WITH DRIED FRUIT

Servings: 4

To banish the grey skies of a winter day, plan an orange dinner party. Begin with Frosty Pumpkin Bisque, *page 113, serve this golden chicken dish as the main course and end with* Baked Apricot Snow, *page 145.*

2 whole chicken breasts, split and skin removed
1 cup plain, nonfat yogurt
1/4 cup frozen orange juice concentrate
1/2 tsp. cinnamon
1/2 tsp. ground coriander

1/2 tsp. turmeric
1 tsp. finely chopped fresh ginger
2–3 cloves garlic, minced or mashed
1/2 small red onion, finely chopped
1/4 cup chopped dried apricots
1/4 cup golden raisins

Preheat oven to 350°. Place chicken parts in a shallow baking pan. Combine yogurt, orange juice concentrate, cinnamon, coriander, turmeric, ginger, garlic, onion and fruit; spoon over chicken. Bake for 45 to 50 minutes or until chicken is brown and cooked through. Spoon any remaining juices and fruit over chicken and serve warm.

per serving *285 calories, 38 g protein, 28 g carb., 2.3 g fat, 83 mg cholesterol, 137 mg sodium*

COLD CHICKEN WITH MUSTARD-TOMATO SAUCE Servings: 4

Leftover chicken or turkey may be substituted for the cold, poached chicken.

1 cup unsalted, defatted chicken stock
2 whole chicken breasts, skin removed
1/2 cup plain, nonfat yogurt
1/4 cup nonfat or reduced-fat mayonnaise
2 tbs. coarse ground, unsalted, prepared mustard
2 tbs. *Peach Chutney,* page 33
1 medium tomato, finely chopped

Pour stock into a skillet that will hold chicken in one layer. Bring stock to a boil, add chicken, cover and simmer until chicken is no longer pink, about 10 to 15 minutes. Remove from pan and cool chicken in refrigerator. In a small bowl, combine remaining ingredients, cover and refrigerate. To serve, slice chicken and cover with sauce.

per serving *195 calories, 35 g protein, 2 g carb., 1.8 g fat, 82 mg cholesterol, 238 mg sodium*

CRUNCHY OVEN-BAKED CHICKEN

Servings: 4

If nonfat bread crumbs are not available, substitute a mixture of cornmeal and whole wheat flour or make your own from fat-free bread or crackers.

1 cup fat-free bread crumbs
1/2 tsp. dried oregano
1/2 tsp. dried basil
1/2 tsp. paprika
1/4 tsp. minced dried garlic
1 tsp. minced dried onion

freshly ground pepper to taste
1 egg white, lightly beaten, or reduced fat egg product to equal
1 whole egg
2 whole chicken breasts, skin removed, split into halves

Preheat oven to 375°. In a shallow bowl, combine bread crumbs, oregano, basil, paprika, garlic, onion and pepper. In another bowl, place egg white or egg product. Dip each piece of chicken in egg, and then in bread crumb mixture. Place chicken on a shallow pan that has been lightly coated with nonstick spray. Bake uncovered for 1 hour or until chicken is brown. Turn once so that chicken browns on all sides.

per serving 256 calories, 37 g protein, 18 g carb., 3 g fat, 83 mg cholesterol, 184 mg sodium

BREAST OF CHICKEN WITH ORANGE SAUCE

Servings: 4

Wine, ginger and curry flavors make a delicious, nutritious company favorite. If you don't have a flame-proof pan, transfer cooked chicken to serving platter and make sauce in a skillet.

1 small onion, finely chopped
1 medium carrot, grated
1/2 green or red bell pepper, chopped
1 tbs. grated orange zest or dried orange bits
2 whole chicken breasts, split and skin removed
1 cup orange juice

1/4 cup dry white wine
1/4 cup unsalted, defatted chicken stock
1 tsp. grated fresh ginger
2 tsp. curry powder
1 tsp. low-sodium soy sauce
1 tbs. cornstarch dissolved in 2 tbs. water
orange slices for garnish

Preheat oven to 350°. Place onion, carrot, pepper and orange zest in bottom of a shallow flame-proof baking pan that will hold chicken in one layer. Arrange chicken breasts on top of vegetables. Combine 1/2 cup orange juice, wine, and stock; pour over chicken. Cover and bake 30 minutes or until chicken is cooked through. Remove chicken from pan and keep warm. Add remaining orange juice, ginger, curry powder, soy sauce and cornstarch to pan; mix with chicken juices. Heat until sauce begins to thicken. Pour sauce over chicken and garnish with orange slices.

per serving *228 calories, 34 g protein, 14 g carb., 2.2 g fat, 82 mg cholesterol, 171 mg sodium*

CHICKEN AND TORTILLA CASSEROLE

Servings: 8

Baked, unsalted, bagged tortillas chips are now appearing in most supermarkets or specialty grocery stores. They may be substituted for the corn tortillas.

8 corn tortillas
1 cup canned stewed tomatoes or salsa, no
   salt added
1 cup plain, nonfat yogurt
1 can (3½ oz.) diced green chiles

1 tbs. chili powder
cloves garlic, minced or mashed
1 small onion, finely chopped
3 cups diced cooked chicken or turkey
2 cups grated, nonfat cheddar cheese

Preheat oven to 350°. Place tortillas on oven rack and heat until crisp. Combine tomatoes, yogurt, chiles, chili powder, garlic and onion. Place half of toasted tortillas in the bottom of a 9x13-inch shallow casserole pan that has been lightly coated with nonstick cooking spray. Cover with a layer of sauce, chicken and cheese. Repeat layers, ending with cheese. Bake uncovered 25 to 30 minutes.

per serving 234 calories, 26.9 g protein, 19.4 g carb., 5 g fat, 52 mg cholesterol, 261 mg sodium

CHICKEN AND POTATOES

Potatoes were originally grown in the mountains of Peru. Explorers who went to the New World looking for gold found potatoes. The explorers might have preferred the former, but potatoes, which fed millions, were more valuable.

3–4 medium potatoes, sliced 1/2-inch thick
4 drumsticks with thighs attached, skin removed
1 medium onion, thinly sliced

2 cloves garlic, minced or mashed
1/4 cup chopped fresh basil
1/4 cup chopped fresh parsley
2 medium tomatoes, chopped

Preheat oven to 375°. Spray a shallow 10-inch baking dish with nonstick spray. Place potatoes on bottom; top with chicken parts. Scatter onions, garlic, basil, parsley and tomatoes over chicken. Cover and bake for 45 minutes or until chicken and potatoes are cooked. Uncover pan and using tongs or a fork, lift up chicken pieces so that they are on top. Return pan to oven and continue baking until chicken is brown.

per serving 367 calories, 39.3 g protein,
39.4 g carb., 6.8 g fat, 142 mg cholesterol, 164 mg sodium

CHICKEN SIMMERED WITH PEACHES

Servings: 4

Historians believe that peach trees were first grown in ancient China about 3000 years ago. Golden peaches became a symbol of immortality.

2 tbs. unbleached white flour
2 tbs. finely chopped fresh basil
1 tsp. dry mustard
8–10 grinds black pepper
1 whole chicken breast, split, skin removed
4 chicken thighs, skin removed

1/4 cup unsalted, defatted chicken stock or nonstick spray,
2 green onions, finely chopped
1–2 cloves garlic, minced or mashed
1/2 cup white wine
2 small fresh peaches, seeded and chopped

Combine flour, basil, mustard and pepper in a paper bag. Add chicken pieces and shake to coat. Heat 1 tbs. stock in a nonstick skillet or lightly coat pan with nonstick spray; slowly brown chicken on all sides. If chicken begins to stick, add chicken stock 1 tablespoon at a time. Push chicken to the side and in the same pan cook green onions and garlic until onions are soft. Add wine, remaining stock and peaches to pan. Cover and simmer until chicken is done; uncover and simmer until sauce is thick.

per serving 265 calories, 39.4 g protein, 8 g carb., 5.3 g fat, 135 mg cholesterol, 122 mg sodium

TURKEY BREAST WITH SHERRY

Adding a small amount of flavored liquid when cooking turkey breasts helps to avoid dried-out meat. Chicken broth may be substituted for sherry, and oregano for cinnamon.

1 turkey breast, approximately 3 lb.
1 small onion, sliced
juice of 1/2 lemon
1/4 cup dry sherry

2 dashes of Angostura bitters, optional
1/2 tsp. cinnamon
4–6 grinds black pepper

Preheat oven to 350°. Remove any webbing or string from turkey; discard visible fat. Line a small roasting pan with a large sheet of heavy-duty aluminum foil. Lay onion slices on foil; place turkey on top, meaty side up. Combine lemon juice, sherry, bitters and cinnamon; spoon over turkey. Season with black pepper. Bring up sides of foil and roll them over to seal the package. Crimp ends. Bake for 20 minutes per pound or until turkey is no longer pink when pierced with a knife at the thickest part. Open foil the last 20 minutes so that breast will brown.

per serving *193 calories, 29 g protein, 1.3 g carb., 6.3 g fat, 72 mg cholesterol, 702 mg sodium*

CHICKEN DIJONNAISE

A mustard coating gives chicken a tangy flavor and golden brown covering. Guests will never care that the skin is missing.

2 whole chicken breasts, cut in half, skin and fat removed
1/4 cup mustard (use 1/2 Dijon and 1/2 coarse grain mustard)
freshly ground pepper to taste
1/3 cup white wine
1/2 cup low-fat ricotta cheese, or 1/4 cup ricotta and 1/4 cup nonfat yogurt
1 cup seedless red grapes

Coat chicken with mustard and set it in a flame-proof baking pan. Cover and marinate at room temperature for 30 minutes, or overnight in the refrigerator. Season with pepper and pour wine around chicken. Bake, uncovered, in preheated oven for 30 to 40 minutes, basting occasionally. Remove chicken to serving platter, cover and keep warm; stir cheese or combine cheese and yogurt into mustard drippings. Simmer sauce for 5 minutes. Add grapes and mix for 1 minute. Spoon over chicken.

per serving *250 calories, 33 g protein, 13.1 g carb., 7.2 g fat, 75 mg cholesterol, 114 mg sodium*

CURRIED CHICKEN

Serve the sauce over rice and surround it with the chicken and fruit.

2 whole chicken breasts, cut in half, or 4
   thighs, skin removed
2 tbs. curry powder
1 medium onion, chopped
2 cloves garlic, finely chopped
1 can sliced water chestnuts
1 medium-sized green apple, diced

1 small banana, diced
1/2 cup canned chunk pineapple, no sugar
   added
1 tbs. tomato paste
1 cup defatted chicken stock
mint leaves for garnish, if available

Lightly coat skillet with nonstick olive oil spray. Slowly brown chicken. Sprinkle with curry powder. Remove chicken and set aside. Add onions, garlic and water chestnuts to pan; stir and cook for 3 minutes. Add apple, banana, pineapple, tomato paste and chicken stock. Return chicken to pan. Cover and cook for 20 minutes. Uncover and cook for 15 minutes.

per serving *275 calories, 30 g protein, 32 g carb., 3 g fat, 70 mg cholesterol, 154 mg sodium*

CHICKEN WITH MANDARIN ORANGES

Servings: 4

No one ever has too many chicken recipes. This one is quick and colorful.

2 tbs. whole-wheat flour
1/2 tsp. dried basil
1/2 tsp. paprika
freshly ground black pepper to taste
2 whole chicken breast, boned, skinned and split (4 pieces)

1/2 cup non-fat, unsalted chicken broth
2 cloves garlic, minced or mashed, or 1/2 garlic purée
1/2 tsp. dry mustard
1/2 cup dry white wine
1 cup mandarin oranges, canned without sugar

Combine flour, basil, paprika and pepper in a paper bag. Add chicken pieces and shake to coat. Heat pan, add 1–2 tbs. broth or lightly spray pan with a non-stick olive oil spray. Brown chicken on all sides. Push chicken to side; briefly cook garlic and mustard, 30 seconds. Add wine, and remaining broth, bring to boil, cover and simmer for 15–20 minutes, or until chicken is done. With a slotted spoon, remove chicken to serving dish; keep warm. Add mandarin oranges to pan, raise heat and cook uncovered until sauce is reduced by half. Pour over chicken and serve. Garnish with additional mandarin oranges, if desired.

per serving *171 calories, 28.7 g protein, 9.6 g carb., 2 g fat, 65 mg cholesterol, 270 mg sodium*

SEAFOOD

91 Crunchy Boiled Fish

92 East Indian Baked Fish

93 Creole Baked Fish

94 Cold Baked Salmon for a Party

95 Salmon Mousse

96 Ginger-Orange Fish Steaks

97 Scallops With Chutney Sauce

98 Spicy Broiled Fish

99 Quick and Easy Fish With Orange Sauce

100 Fish and Vegetable Kabobs

102 Baked Fish With Salsa

103 Steamed Clams in Wine

104 Shrimp Curry in Red Pepper Boats

Research shows that the oils from fish may play a role in preventing heart disease. Scientific analysis shows that clams, mussels, scallops and oysters are very low in cholesterol. A 3½ ounce serving of any finned fish or shelled mollusk generally has less than 100 milligrams of cholesterol. Even shrimp and squid, which are higher in cholesterol than other seafood, can still be included if you watch the total cholesterol for the day.

Look for fillets and steaks that appear moist and firm. There should be little evidence of bruising or reddening of the flesh. Pre-packaged fish should contain a minimum of liquid as seafood stored in liquid quickly deteriorates. Make certain that seafood is the last item you purchase. When you get home store fish in the coldest part of the refrigerator; use within two days.

CRUNCHY BROILED FISH

Panko is the name for Japanese-style bread crumbs that are usually made without added shortening. Look for it in the ethnic foods section of the supermarket.

1/2 cup plain nonfat yogurt
1/2 tsp. dry mustard
1/4 tsp. Tabasco Sauce
3/4 cup panko or fat-free bread or cracker
  crumbs

1 tsp. Italian seasoning
1 tsp. minced dried onion
1 1/4 lb. fish fillets

Preheat broiler if necessary. In one plate, combine yogurt, mustard and Tabasco; in another mix together panko, Italian seasoning and dried onions. Dip fillets in yogurt mixture, and then in bread crumbs. Place coated fillets on broiler pan that has been coated with nonstick spray. Broil about 5 minutes; turn and broil for an additional 3 to 5 minutes or until fish is no longer translucent.

per serving *245 calories, 36 g protein, 16.2 g carb., 3 g fat, 83 mg cholesterol, 160 mg sodium*

EAST INDIAN BAKED FISH

Mixing a small amount of flour with yogurt and then baking the fish at high temperature produces a crisp crust. The dish may be prepared in advance, refrigerated and baked just before serving.

2 small, whole fish such as trout or perch, 8 oz. each
juice of 1/2 lemon
nonstick olive oil spray
1 tbs. finely chopped or grated fresh ginger

2–3 cloves garlic, minced or mashed
1 cup plain nonfat yogurt
1 tsp. garam masala (see page 66)
2 tbs. whole wheat flour

Preheat oven to 400°. Rinse fish under running water and remove scales; pat dry. Rub inside of fish with lemon juice. Lightly coat pan with nonstick spray. Heat pan; add ginger and garlic and cook for 30 seconds. Reduce heat and add yogurt, garam masala and flour to pan; simmer 2 to 3 minutes. Place fish in shallow baking pan; cover with yogurt mixture. Bake uncovered for 20 to 25 minutes or until inside of fish is no longer translucent and crust is crisp and brown.

per serving *177 calories, 26.3 g protein, 8.3 g carb., 3.9 g fat, 63 mg cholesterol, 73 mg sodium*

CREOLE BAKED FISH

Now that canned, stewed tomatoes are available without added salt, a spicy baked fish dish can be ready in minutes. Be careful with the cayenne—it's hot!

1¼ lb. fish fillets
1 can (14½ oz.) unsalted stewed tomatoes
2 tsp. dried basil
½ red or green bell pepper, chopped
1 small onion, chopped
1–2 ribs celery, chopped
¼ tsp. cayenne pepper (or less, to taste)

Preheat oven to 400°. Place fish fillets in a shallow baking dish, big enough to hold fish in one layer. Combine remaining ingredients and pour over fish. Bake covered for about 15 minutes. Remove fish to serving platter and spoon juices and vegetables over fish.

per serving *159 calories, 27.8 g protein, 7.3 g carb., 1.9 g fat, 68 mg cholesterol, 131 mg sodium*

COLD BAKED SALMON FOR A PARTY

Fish is considered done when it is no longer translucent. For a whole fish, allow 15 minutes cooking time per inch of thickness, measured at the thickest portion.

3 lb. whole salmon
heavy duty foil
juice of half a lemon
2–3 sprigs parsley
4–6 grinds of black pepper

1 cup plain nonfat yogurt
1 small cucumber, peeled and grated
1 tbs. chopped fresh dill weed or 1 tsp. dried
6–8 cherry tomatoes

Preheat oven to 425°. Rinse fish under running water and pat dry with paper towels. Cut a piece of foil large enough to wrap fish, allowing for some overlap. Lay fish in middle of foil and sprinkle with lemon juice. Tuck parsley in cavity of fish and rub with black pepper. Wrap foil around fish tightly so juices will not run. Place fish on a baking sheet and bake until fish is opaque when cut near the center, about 30 to 40 minutes. While fish is baking, combine yogurt, cucumber and fresh dill. Cover and refrigerate until serving time. Spoon yogurt sauce over fish at serving time and garnish with tomatoes.

---

per serving *333 calories, 36.1 g protein, 4.8 g carb., 17.9 g fat, 113 mg cholesterol, 105 mg sodium*

SALMON MOUSSE

A club woman we know says that this mousse is her favorite choice for board or committee lunches. She unmolds and garnishes the mousse ahead of time so that it can wait in the refrigerator until serving time.

1 envelope unflavored gelatin
1/4 cup cold water
1/4 cup boiling water
2 tbs. lemon juice
1/2 small onion, chopped
1/4 tsp. paprika
1 tsp. dill weed

dash Tabasco Sauce
2 cups cooked fresh salmon or canned red salmon
1 cup plain nonfat yogurt
cherry tomatoes and thinly sliced cucumber as garnish

Dissolve gelatin in cold water; pour into food processor or blender. Add boiling water, lemon juice, onion, paprika, dill weed and Tabasco; process 30 seconds. Add salmon and yogurt and process until smooth. Pour mixture into a 4- to 6-cup mold. Cover and chill for at least 4 hours. Unmold on a serving platter and garnish with cherry tomatoes and thin slices of cucumber.

per 1/4 recipe *227 calories, 28 g protein, 5.9 g carb., 9.4 g fat, 75 mg cholesterol, 101 mg sodium*

GINGER-ORANGE FISH STEAKS

Many unusual species of seafood are now appearing at fish markets. We like Mahi-Mahi, orange roughy, tuna and marlin. If your fish market does not have them, substitute any strongly flavored fish steaks.

1 tbs. orange juice concentrate
1 tbs. unsalted, Dijon-style mustard
1 tsp. dry mustard
2 tsp. grated fresh ginger
2 tsp. balsamic vinegar

1 tsp. reduced-sodium soy sauce
1 tsp. toasted sesame seeds
1 1/2 lb. fish steaks or thick fillets
freshly ground pepper to taste

Preheat oven to 450°. Combine juice concentrate, mustards, ginger, vinegar, soy sauce, and sesame seeds in shallow pan. Place fish in pan and spoon orange mixture over all. Bake for about 15 minutes, or until fish is opaque at the thickest part. Season with pepper and serve.

per serving *155 calories, 30.8 g protein, 2.4 g carb., 1.7 g fat, 73 mg cholesterol, 141 mg sodium*

SCALLOPS WITH CHUTNEY SAUCE

Servings: 4

To keep scallops tender and sweet, sear quickly over high heat. This technique seals in the juices. Scallops will be tough if overcooked.

1/2 cup chutney
2 tbs. rice vinegar
1 lb. scallops, cut in half if large
2 cloves garlic, minced or mashed
1 tbs. minced fresh ginger

1 small dried red chile, seeded and minced
   or 1/4 tsp. crushed red pepper flakes
2 cups hot cooked converted rice
1 tsp. toasted sesame seeds
2–3 green onions, finely chopped

Combine chutney and vinegar; set aside. Lightly coat a pan with nonstick spray. Heat pan and stir-fry scallops, garlic, ginger and chile peppers for 2 to 3 minutes. Remove scallops from pan and keep warm. Add chutney mixture and bring the mixture to a boil. Reduce heat and simmer uncovered for 4 to 5 minutes. Return scallops to pan and heat through, about 3 to 4 minutes. Serve warm over rice and garnish with sesame seeds and onions.

per serving *486 calories, 26.7 g protein, 86.9 g carb., 2.3 g fat, 38 mg cholesterol, 192 mg sodium*

SPICY BROILED FISH

Fish has very little connective tissue and requires a short cooking time. When broiling, the fish should be approximately 4 inches from the heat source; too close and the fish may burn; too far away and it will cook unevenly.

1/4 cup plain, nonfat yogurt
1/4 cup nonfat mayonnaise
1 tsp. unsalted, dijon-style mustard
2 cloves garlic, minced or mashed
1 tsp. dried tarragon
1 1/2 lb. fish steaks

Preheat broiler if necessary. Combine yogurt, mayonnaise, mustard, garlic and tarragon. Place fish in a broiler pan. Spoon yogurt mixture over fish and broil about 5 minutes; turn and broil for an additional 5 to 7 minutes or until fish is no longer translucent.

per serving *185 calories, 31.3 g protein, 4 g carb., 4.1 g fat, 77 mg cholesterol, 194 mg sodium*

QUICK AND EASY FISH WITH ORANGE SAUCE

Servings: 4

When we were first learning to cook without fat, we developed this quick and easy fish sauce. Our families still rate it as their favorite fish dish.

1½ lb. fish fillets
2 tbs. frozen orange juice concentrate
¼ cup dry sherry

½ tsp. grated fresh ginger
½ tsp. dry mustard
1 tsp. low-sodium soy sauce

Place fish fillets in a shallow baking pan. Combine remaining ingredients and pour over fish. Cover and refrigerate for 30 minutes. Preheat broiler if necessary. Broil 4 inches from source of heat until fish is no longer translucent.

per serving *187 calories, 32.3 g protein, 3.6 g carb., 2 g fat, 85 mg cholesterol, 140 mg sodium*

VARIATION

Add 1 to 2 cloves of garlic, minced or mashed and 1 tsp. unsalted, Dijon-style mustard

FISH AND VEGETABLE KABOBS

For an informal gathering, let your guests create their own combinations of vegetables. Any firm fish or combination of vegetables can be used in this tasty, spicy sauce. To prevent burning, soak wooden skewers in water before using.

3/4 cup plain nonfat yogurt
2 tsp. grated ginger root
1–2 cloves garlic, minced or mashed
1 tsp. dry mustard
1 tbs. lemon juice
2 tsp. curry powder
1/2 tsp. ground cumin
1/4 tsp. turmeric
1/4 tsp. crushed red pepper flakes
1 lb. white fish cut into 2-inch pieces or 1 lb. large scallops
12 whole mushrooms
12 cherry tomatoes
1/2 each red, yellow and green bell peppers, cut into 2-inch pieces

In a large bowl, combine yogurt, ginger, garlic, mustard, lemon juice and spices. Add fish, cover and marinate in refrigerator for several hours. Remove fish, reserving yogurt mixture. Thread fish on skewers; thread vegetables on separate skewers. Grill or broil skewers of fish and vegetables, starting with those that take the longest. Baste occasionally with yogurt marinade.

per serving *171 calories, 26 g protein, 12.6 g carb., 2 g fat, 55 mg cholesterol, 135 mg sodium*

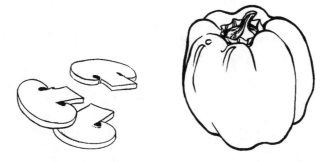

BAKED FISH WITH SALSA

Since this dish has a flavorful sauce, we suggest using a plain white fish, such as flounder, cod or rock fish.

3/4 cup plain, nonfat yogurt
1/4 cup nonfat or reduced-fat mayonnaise
1 tbs. whole wheat flour
1/2 cup unsalted salsa
1 1/2 lb. firm fish fillets
1 small tomato, sliced

Heat oven to 400°. In a shallow baking dish that will hold the fillets in one layer, mix together yogurt, mayonnaise, flour and salsa. Add fillets and arrange tomato slices on top. Spoon sauce over tomatoes, making certain that fillets are well covered. Bake uncovered for about 20 minutes or until fish is no longer translucent when pierced with a knife.

---

per serving 238 calories, 35.3 g protein, 9.8 g carb., 5.8 g fat, 86 mg cholesterol, 276 mg sodium

STEAMED CLAMS IN WINE

Servings: 4

Before cooking, clams should be tightly closed or close immediately when tapped. Clams will then open when cooked in a steaming broth. Serve hot with plenty of sourdough bread for dunking. Mussels may be substituted for the clams.

2 lb. clams
1 cup white wine
1/2 cup finely chopped red onion
2–3 cloves garlic, minced or mashed
1/4 tsp. crushed red pepper flakes
2–3 dashes Tabasco Sauce

Scrub clams; discard any that have chipped or cracked shells. Combine wine, onion, garlic, crushed red pepper and Tabasco in a large pan. Bring to a boil, reduce heat and simmer 2 to 3 minutes. Add clams, cover and steam until clams have opened. Discard any that do not open.

per serving *77 calories, 13 g protein, 3 g carb., 0.8 g fat, 33 mg cholesterol, 89 mg sodium*

SHRIMP CURRY IN RED PEPPER BOATS

Servings: 10–12

This makes a colorful appetizer or low-fat snack.

1 cup cooked tiny shrimp, reserve 16 for
    garnish
2 tbs. reduced-calorie mayonnaise
1 tbs. nonfat yogurt
2 tsp. fruit concentrate
2 green onions, thinly sliced

$1/8$ cup slivered almonds, finely chopped
$1/2$ cup golden raisins
1–2 tsp. curry powder
$1/2$ tsp. dry mustard
2 red bell peppers, cut in half lengthwise
    and seeded

Combine shrimp and remaining ingredients except peppers. Cut each half of red pepper into eight bite-sized pieces and place on serving dish. Top each with a tsp. of shrimp mixture and garnish with reserved shrimp. Serve immediately or cover with plastic wrap and refrigerate for up to 8 hours.

per serving *88 calories, 5.5 g protein, 9.1 g carb., 3.4 g fat, 46 mg cholesterol, 54 mg sodium*

SOUPS

106 Vegetable Soup
107 Lentil Soup
108 Tomato and Barley Soup
109 Chilled Dilled Soup
110 Mushroom and Tarragon Soup
111 Cool and Refreshing Fruit Soup

112 Cold Zucchini Soup
113 Frosty Pumpkin Bisque in a Pumpkin
     Soup Bowl
114 Spring Green Asparagus Soup
115 Chicken and Tofu Soup

An old encyclopedia had this to say about soup: "From a dietetic point of view we may regard soups as gastric stimulants and as articles of nutrition." Time has not altered this definition. Soups are wonderful dishes that can be useful for any meal: breakfast, lunch or dinner. They provide a way to use up all those bits and pieces of leftover foods. They can be stored in the refrigerator or freezer for quick unplanned meals. Hot soups are a soothing comfort on a cold afternoon; cold soups have a calming effect on a hot evening. Next time you need a break on a hectic day, try soup instead of a more stimulating drink.

VEGETABLE SOUP

There is no one recipe for vegetable soup. The vegetables will depend on the season and your taste; the proportions are only a guide, so substitute freely. For a thicker soup add more vegetables, pasta, potatoes or grains.

8 cups unsalted, defatted chicken or
    vegetable stock
2 small carrots, chopped
3–4 ribs celery with leaves, chopped
1 medium onion, chopped
2–3 cloves garlic, minced or mashed
1 tsp. dry mustard
1/4 lb. fresh or frozen green beans

1–2 small yellow squash, chopped
1 cup cooked white or red beans
2 tbs. tomato paste without salt
2 cups fresh or frozen corn
3–4 sprigs parsley, chopped
3–4 basil leaves, chopped
freshly ground pepper to taste

In a large soup pot, combine stock, carrots, celery, onion, garlic, mustard, green beans, squash, beans and tomato paste. Bring to a boil, reduce heat and simmer covered for 30 minutes. Add corn, parsley, basil and pepper. Simmer uncovered for 20 minutes. Serve hot.

per serving *106 calories, 4.6 g protein, 48.8 g carb., 1.3 g fat, 2 mg cholesterol, 36 mg sodium*

LENTIL SOUP

Several years ago, the Center for Science in the Public Interest featured this recipe on one of their Christmas cards. We think you will agree that it is a winner.

7–8 cups unsalted, defatted chicken or
    vegetable stock
2 cups dried lentils, rinsed
2 medium onions, chopped
3–4 cloves garlic, minced or mashed
1 tsp. dry mustard
2 carrots, chopped
3–4 ribs celery with tops, chopped

1–2 small potatoes, diced
2–3 sprigs parsley
1 bay leaf
4–6 fresh basil leaves, chopped or 1 tsp.
    dried
1/4 tsp. cayenne pepper
1 tbs. dried tomato bits, optional
freshly ground pepper to taste

In a large soup pot, combine stock, lentils, onions, garlic, mustard, carrots, celery, potatoes, parsley, bay leaf, basil, cayenne pepper and dried tomatoes. Bring to a boil, cover and simmer about 1 hour. Add freshly ground pepper. Remove bay leaf and parsley before serving.

per serving *213 calories, 14.7 g protein, 65.3 g carb., 1 g fat, 2 mg cholesterol, 32 mg sodium*

TOMATO AND BARLEY SOUP

Barley, an old world grain, combines with tomatoes, a new world fruit, in this very tasty soup. To vary, add 1 cup sliced fresh mushrooms to soup just before serving.

6 cups unsalted, defatted chicken or vegetable stock
1/2 cup barley
1 medium onion, chopped
2–3 ribs celery including leaves, chopped
3 medium tomatoes, chopped
4–6 black peppercorns
1 tbs. low-sodium soy sauce
4–6 basil leaves, chopped, or 1 tsp. dried
1/4 cup reduced acid, frozen orange juice concentrate

In a large soup pot, combine stock, barley, onions, celery, tomatoes, peppercorns, soy sauce, basil and orange juice concentrate. Bring to a boil and simmer covered for 1 to 1 1/2 hours. Serve warm.

per serving *198 calories, 3 g protein, 49.3 g carb., 1.1 g fat, 2 mg cholesterol, 25 mg sodium*

CHILLED DILLED SOUP

Servings: 4

In colonial times children were given dill seeds to chew in church to keep them awake. For this reason dill seeds were known as "meetin' seeds".

2 medium cucumbers, peeled, seeded and chopped
2 green onions, finely chopped
1/2 cup finely chopped, fresh parsley
1/2 cup chopped, fresh dill weed
1/2 tsp. ground coriander
2–3 drops Tabasco Sauce
2 cups plain, nonfat yogurt
1 cup nonfat, lemon yogurt
dill sprigs or lemon slices for garnish

Combine all ingredients except garnish in food processor. Process briefly until smooth. Turn mixture into bowl, cover and chill 2 to 3 hours. Garnish with fresh dill or lemon slices.

per serving *124 calories, 11.3 g protein, 19.7 g carb., 0.6 g fat, 3 mg cholesterol, 141 mg sodium*

MUSHROOM AND TARRAGON SOUP

Use our cream substitute in all your old recipes calling for whipped or heavy cream. The "cream" keeps in the refrigerator for up to ten days and the recipe is easily doubled.

1 lb. fresh mushrooms
4 cups unsalted, defatted chicken or vegetable stock
1/4 cup lightly packed fresh tarragon leaves or 1 tbs.
  dried
1/2 cup *Substitute Cream,* page 15

Combine mushrooms and broth in a food processor
or blender; process until mushrooms are finely chopped.
You may need to do this in 2 batches. Pour mushrooms, broth
and tarragon leaves into a 3- to 4-quart saucepan. Bring to a boil, cover and simmer about
10 minutes. Stir in "cream" and serve hot.

per serving *including cream substitute 134 calories,
10.4 g protein, 38.7 g carb., 5.9 g fat, 21 mg cholesterol, 97 mg sodium*

COOL AND REFRESHING FRUIT SOUP

In the summertime we keep a big bowl of this soup in the refrigerator. It is a healthful snack any time of day. With so many fresh fruits and frozen fruit juice concentrates to choose from, you can have different flavors every time.

3 tbs. instant tapioca
2½ cups water
1 can (6 oz.) blended fruit juice concentrate
3 cups fresh fruit (melons, oranges, nectarines, peaches and bananas are good choices, but use whatever is in season)
fresh mint

Combine tapioca and 1 cup of water in a medium saucepan. Bring mixture to a boil and simmer uncovered for 2 to 3 minutes. Add orange juice and mix until well blended. Add remaining water. Cover and refrigerate until cold. Cut fruit into bite-sized pieces; add to soup. Serve in chilled mugs. Garnish with fresh mint.

per serving *134 calories, 2 g protein, 32.5 g carb., 0.4 g fat, 0 mg cholesterol, 12 mg sodium*

COLD ZUCCHINI SOUP

Servings: 2

The hottest summer day can be improved by a cup of chilled soup. And, as anyone who has ever grown zucchini will tell you, you can never have enough recipes for zucchini.

1 cup sliced zucchini
2 cloves garlic, minced or mashed
1/2 cup nonfat milk
1 cup plain nonfat yogurt

Place all ingredients in food processor or blender; process until smooth. Pour into bowl and place in refrigerator until chilled. Serve cold.

per serving 98 calories, 9.5 g protein, 14.5 g carb., 0.4 g fat, 3 mg cholesterol, 121 mg sodium

FROSTY PUMPKIN BISQUE IN A PUMPKIN SOUP BOWL

Servings: 6

A carved-out pumpkin serves as a soup bowl for this autumn favorite. Look for a pumpkin that has a smooth skin and no blemishes. Cut off the top and scrape out the insides. Rub a small amount of oil on the outside to give the bowl a shiny look.

1 cup low-fat, low-sodium ricotta cheese
1 can (16 oz.) pumpkin
2 cups unsalted, defatted chicken stock

1/3 cup nonfat sour cream
2 tbs. chopped chives

Combine ricotta cheese and pumpkin in a food processor or blender and purée until mixture is smooth. Pour into a medium soup pot and add chicken stock. Bring to a boil, reduce heat and simmer uncovered for 2 to 3 minutes. Stir in sour cream and chives. Pour into a bowl, cover and chill until serving time. Garnish with extra sour cream and chives.

per serving 93 calories, 6.3 g protein, 18.9 g carb., 3.7 g fat, 14 mg cholesterol, 66 mg sodium

SPRING GREEN ASPARAGUS SOUP

Servings: 4

Until the 20th century asparagus was commonly called sparrow-grass or grass. For variation, before adding milk, purée soup in a food processor or blender and then proceed with the recipe.

2 cups unsalted, defatted chicken or
    vegetable stock
1 medium potato, diced
3–4 ribs celery with tops, chopped
1 small onion, chopped

1½ lb. fresh asparagus, cut into 2- to 3-inch
    pieces
1 cup nonfat milk
freshly grated nutmeg to taste
freshly ground pepper to taste

In a medium saucepan, combine stock, potato, celery and onion. Cook mixture over medium heat until vegetables are soft. Add asparagus, reserving 4 to 6 small tips for garnish. Continue cooking until asparagus is soft, about 10 minutes. Stir in milk and season with nutmeg and pepper. Garnish with reserved asparagus tips.

per serving 127 calories, 8.9 g protein, 37.9 g carb., 0.9 g fat, 2 mg cholesterol, 68 mg sodium

CHICKEN AND TOFU SOUP

Servings: 4

Just a few years ago tofu (bean curd) was unknown outside of Asian markets. Now it is a standard item in many supermarkets. This marvelous food is a complete protein, so it is no wonder it has been a staple food for centuries.

2–3 dry mushrooms
1/4 cup dry sherry
4 cups well-flavored unsalted, defatted
   chicken or vegetable stock
1 cup sliced fresh mushrooms

2–3 sprigs fresh parsley
1/2 cup cooked chicken, cut into 1-inch
   slices
8 oz. tofu, drained
1 cup edible pea pods

Marinate dry mushrooms in sherry for 30 minutes; drain and chop, reserving liquid. Bring stock to a boil; add dried mushrooms, reserved liquid, fresh mushrooms, parsley, chicken and tofu. Simmer uncovered for 15 minutes. Add pea pods and simmer 5 minutes. Remove parsley stems and serve warm.

per serving *138 calories, 11.8 g protein, 36.6 g carb., 4.8 g fat, 18 mg cholesterol, 29 mg sodium*

VEGETABLES

117 Cooking Methods for Vegetables
118 Baked Beets
118 Baked Onions
118 Oven-Baked Vegetable Chips
119 Sauces for Vegetables
119   Zesty Marinade
119   Tangy Dressing
120 Colorful Vegetable Stew
121 Rosy Red Slaw

122 Marinated Vegetables
123 Cool Summer Salad
124 Double Orange Sweet Potatoes With
         Pears
125 Cheesy Kale
126 Winter Vegetable Casserole
127 Sweet and Creamy Squash
128 Beet Salad With Corn

STORING AND COOKING VEGETABLES

Fresh vegetables remain tasty longer if they are stored properly. Most vegetables should be refrigerated in the crisper or in plastic bags. Mushrooms (which are a fungus) should be refrigerated in a paper bag. Vegetables in pods, like fresh peas or lima beans, should be left in their pods in the refrigerator until just before cooking. Keep dry onions, potatoes, parsnips and winter squash in a cool, dark, dry place—but not in the refrigerator!

Don't assume that all vegetables should be peeled before cooking and eating. Most of the vitamins and minerals in vegetables are just under the skins. Skins also provide fiber. Wash vegetables, scrape or trim as needed, but do not soak. Cook in the smallest amount of water and the shortest time possible. The more liquid you use and the longer the cooking time, the greater the vitamin loss. Cuts also leak nutrients; cook vegetables whole if possible, and cut after cooking. Do not add soda or salt to the liquid.

COOKING METHODS FOR VEGETABLES

STEAMING: Pour water or other liquid into a saucepan to a depth of 1 inch. Place vegetables in a steamer rack and lower into pan. Liquid should not touch vegetables. Bring to a boil, cover, reduce heat and steam until vegetables are crisp and tender—time will depend on size and type of vegetables, but steaming generally takes longer than cooking in liquid. Steam green vegetables uncovered for a few minutes at the start of cooking to keep their bright green color. Serve steamed vegetables plain, with lemon juice and/or herbs, or with a sauce. Some nonfat salad dressings make good sauces for steamed vegetables.

BAKING: Potatoes aren't the only vegetable that can be baked. For variety, serve an entire dinner of baked onions, beets, carrots, sweet potatoes and even garlic. Serve baked vegetables whole or cut into strips or slices, and dressed with a sauce, a favorite salt-free seasoning blend or plain.

BAKED BEETS

Heat oven to 375°. Wash beets thoroughly but do not scrub. (Beets must be treated gently; bruises will cause beet juices to leak out.) Cut off the root and leaves, but leave 1 or 2 inches of stem. Wrap each beet in foil, or place prepared beets in a shallow pan and cover. Bake for 1 to 1½ hours, or until beets are tender and skin slips off easily. Sweet potatoes, carrots and parsnips may be baked the same way, but they can be scrubbed before baking.

BAKED ONIONS

Heat oven to 350°. Cut both ends from onions and remove loose skin, but do not peel. Wipe with a damp paper towel. Wrap onions individually in foil or place in a shallow baking pan. Bake for 45 minutes or until soft. Serve with or without peel, as you wish.

Bake whole garlic heads like onions. Spread baked garlic on toasted French bread.

OVEN BAKED VEGETABLE CHIPS

Heat oven to 425°. Lightly coat a baking pan with nonstick spray. Choose carrots, parsnips or potatoes. Wash vegetables and slice to uniform thickness, ⅛ to ¼ inch. Arrange slices on baking pan. Bake for 10 to 15 minutes, until chips are golden and done to your liking.

SAUCES FOR VEGETABLES

To flavor vegetables in the steamer, to pour over hot cooked vegetables, or to dress cold vegetables, try some of these sauces.

ZESTY MARINADE Makes ¼ cup

1 tbs. wine vinegar

2 tbs. lemon juice

1 tsp. chopped parsley

2 leaves fresh basil, minced, or ½ tsp. dried

Combine all ingredients and beat well to blend.

per recipe *10 calories, 0.1 g protein, 3.6 g carb., 0 g fat, 0 mg cholesterol, 1 mg sodium*

TANGY DRESSING Makes 1 cup

3 tbs. cider or tarragon vinegar

¼ cup plain, nonfat yogurt

2 tbs. finely chopped dried tomato bits

1 clove garlic, minced or mashed

1 tbs. minced fresh tarragon, or 1 tsp. dried

Process all ingredients in a blender container until smooth. Allow to stand several hours for flavors to blend and dressing to thicken.

per ¼ cup *15 calories, 1 g protein, 2.9 g carb., 0.1 g fat, 0 mg cholesterol, 13 mg sodium>*

COLORFUL VEGETABLE STEW

Here's a great stew to serve to your vegetarian friends!

1 lb. tofu
2 tbs. sherry, or substitute lemon juice
2 tbs. balsamic vinegar
1 tbs. low-sodium soy sauce, optional
1/2 cup unsalted, defatted vegetable or chicken stock
1 large onion, chopped
2 cloves garlic, minced or mashed

1 tbs. grated fresh ginger
4 carrots, sliced diagonally
1 red bell pepper, sliced
2 cups sliced yellow squash
2 cups sliced zucchini
2 tbs. unsalted peanut butter
4 cups hot, cooked brown or white rice, or other grain

Slice tofu, press between paper towels to remove liquid, and cut into bite-sized squares. Toss with sherry, vinegar and soy sauce. Set aside. Lightly coat a large skillet with nonstick spray or heat 2 tablespoons stock in a nonstick skillet. Stir-fry vegetables, beginning with onion, garlic and ginger. When onion is soft, add carrots. Cook for 5 minutes; then add red pepper. Cook for 1 minute; then add squash. Add stock as necessary. When vegetables are tender-crisp (about 5 minutes) drain tofu, reserving marinade, and add to vegetables. Heat through. Combine marinade with peanut butter and stir into vegetables. Serve over rice.

per serving 433 calories, 19.1 g protein, 69.2 g carb., 11.7 g fat, 0 mg cholesterol, 51 mg sodium

ROSY RED SLAW

A creamy beet salad is a Christmas tradition in some families of Russian origin. With a food processor, our version goes together in minutes!

1/4 cup red wine vinegar
1 tsp. unsalted Dijon-style mustard
1–2 tsp. fresh or dried dill weed
1 clove garlic, minced or mashed
freshly ground pepper to taste
1 cup nonfat sour cream or plain, nonfat
  yogurt

2 medium beets, cooked, peeled and
  shredded
2 cups shredded red cabbage
1 medium red onion, shredded
2 cups cooked or reduced-sodium canned
  red kidney beans, drained

In a blender or food processor, blend vinegar, mustard, dill, garlic, pepper and sour cream. Set aside. In a large bowl, combine beets, cabbage, onion and beans. Gently stir in sour cream dressing. Cover and refrigerate 2 hours or as long as overnight. Stir again before serving.

per serving *120 calories, 8.1 g protein, 22 g carb., 0.5 g fat, 1 mg cholesterol, 55 mg sodium*

MARINATED VEGETABLES

When you know you're going to be too busy to prepare fresh salad, make these ahead of time and keep in the 'fridge. If you're <u>really</u> swamped, buy the veggies already cut at the salad bar.

2–3 carrots, sliced

1 zucchini, sliced

1/2 green or red bell pepper, diced

1 cup cauliflower, cut into bite-sized pieces

1 cup broccoli, cut into bite-sized pieces

2–3 radishes, sliced

10–15 cherry tomatoes

In a large bowl, combine all vegetables. Mix marinade ingredients and pour over vegetables. Stir gently to coat. Cover and refrigerate for several hours.

MARINADE

1/4 cup dry white wine or wine vinegar

1 cup plain, nonfat yogurt

1–2 cloves garlic, minced or mashed

1 tbs. minced fresh oregano, or 1 tsp. dried

1 tbs. minced fresh basil, or 1 tsp. dried

per serving 98 calories, 6.2 g protein, 16.9 g carb., 0.7 g fat, 1 mg cholesterol, 77 mg sodium

COOL SUMMER SALAD

For a change of flavor, substitute dill or chives for mint.

2 cucumbers, sliced
1/4 lb. fresh mushrooms, sliced
2–3 radishes, sliced
1–2 green onions, chopped
1 cup plain, nonfat yogurt or nonfat sour cream
1–2 cloves garlic, minced or mashed
2 tbs. minced fresh mint, or 1 tsp. dried
2 tbs. lemon juice
freshly ground pepper to taste

Place cucumbers and mushrooms in a colander and set aside to drain. Combine all remaining ingredients. Turn cucumbers and mushrooms into a large bowl and gently stir in yogurt mix. Cover and chill several hours.

per serving 64 calories, 4.9 g protein, 11.6 g carb., 0.5 g fat, 1 mg cholesterol, 49 mg sodium

DOUBLE ORANGE SWEET POTATOES WITH PEARS   Servings: 6

Yams, which in this country are really sweet potatoes, could be substituted. Naturally occurring sugars form the golden crust.

3 sweet potatoes (about 3 lb.), cooked and peeled
2 fresh pears, cored
1/4 cup orange marmalade, sweetened with fruit juices

1 cup unsweetened orange juice
1/2 tsp. cinnamon
1 tbs. finely cut orange zest
1 tbs. rum or 1 tsp. rum flavoring

Preheat oven to 375°. Thinly slice sweet potatoes and pears. Arrange in alternate layers in an 8-inch square baking dish that has been coated with nonstick spray. In a small saucepan, combine remaining ingredients. Heat until marmalade is melted. Pour over potatoes and pears. Bake uncovered for 30 minutes, until top is golden and crusty.

per serving *171 calories, 1.8 g protein, 40.5 g carb., 0.5 g fat, 0 mg cholesterol, 13 mg sodium*

CHEESY KALE

Kale is a nutritionist's dream. One cup of cooked kale contains ample amounts of iron, Vitamin A and Vitamin C, but only 43 calories. Look for crisp green leaves when buying kale; yellow, wilted leaves indicate a vegetable that's past its prime.

1/2 tsp. mustard seeds
2–3 tbs. unsalted, defatted chicken stock
3–4 green onions, sliced
2 cloves garlic, minced or mashed

4 cups washed, chopped kale leaves
1/2 cup low-fat, low-sodium ricotta cheese
1 tbs. grated nonfat Parmesan cheese
freshly ground pepper

Lightly coat a medium skillet with nonstick spray and heat; toast mustard seeds. Add 1 tbs. stock to pan and stir-cook onions and garlic until onions begin to brown. Add 1 to 2 tbs. stock and stir-cook kale 3 to 5 minutes, until softened but not totally wilted. Stir in ricotta and Parmesan cheeses. Season to taste with pepper.

per serving *87 calories, 6.6 g protein, 11.1 g carb., 3 g fat, 13 mg cholesterol, 83 mg sodium*

WINTER VEGETABLE CASSEROLE

Here's a hearty winter main dish that's nearly fat- and cholesterol-free. Serve it with one of our baked fruit desserts for something healthy from the oven that is truly lovin'.

reduced-fat egg product equal to 3 eggs
8 oz. nonfat cream cheese
1 tsp. dry mustard
1 tsp. dried oregano
1/8 tsp. freshly ground black pepper
2 tbs. chopped fresh parsley

2 cloves garlic, minced or mashed
1 medium onion, grated
1 parsnip, peeled and grated
1 rutabaga, peeled and grated
3 baking potatoes, grated

Heat oven to 400°. In a large bowl, combine egg product, cream cheese, mustard, oregano, pepper, parsley and garlic. Add onion, parsnip, rutabaga and potatoes. Mix well. Pour into a 3-quart baking dish that has been coated with nonstick spray. Bake for 1 1/2 hours, or until top is brown and crisp around the edges.

per serving *123 calories, 9 g protein, 20.8 g carb., 0.8 g fat, 5 mg cholesterol, 203 mg sodium*

SWEET AND CREAMY SQUASH

Servings: 4

We recommend Delicata squash but any fresh squash or fresh pumpkin may be substituted.

2 cups peeled and diced Delicata squash
$1/2$ cup ricotta cheese
1 (8 oz.) can crushed pineapple, no sugar added
$1/2$ tsp. ground cinnamon
$1/2$ tsp. freshly grated nutmeg

Combine squash and remaining ingredients in food processor or blender. Purée. To serve, mound the squash on a platter and surround with slices of kiwi, pineapple oranges. Serve or at room temperature.

per serving 88 calories, 4.5 g protein, 10.5 g carb., 2.9 g fat, 10 mg cholesterol, 67 mg sodium

BEET SALAD WITH CORN

Servings: 4

Fresh corn should be cooked 1 or 2 minutes; frozen corn may be added without thawing.

1/4 cup reduced calorie mayonnaise
1/4 cup nonfat yogurt
2 tbs. frozen orange juice concentrate
1/4 cup sliced or chopped red onion
1 tbs. Dijon mustard
1/2 tsp. dill weed
1 cup diced water chestnuts or jicama
2 cups cooked diced beets
1/2 cup fresh or frozen corn

Combine mayonnaise, yogurt, juice concentrate, mustard and dill. Add water chestnuts and beets to salad dressing. Stir in corn.

per serving 237 calories, 4.5 g protein, 27.9 g carb., 12 g fat, 8 mg cholesterol, 86 mg sodium

GRAINS

130 Cooking Times for Grains

131 Red and Green Baked Barley

132 Warm Barley Pudding

133 Millet and Pear Pudding

134 Crunchy Brown Rice

135 Basmati Rice Salad

136 Quinoa Pilaf

137 Creamy Grain Berry Salad With Fruit

The Dietary Recommendations from the National Research Council state that Americans should "increase intake of complex carbohydrates." The best way to reach that goal is to eat more whole grains. There are many to choose from: amaranth, barley, bulgur, corn, millet, oats, quinoa, rice and wheat berries.

WHAT IS A GRAIN?

A grain is a seed made up of three parts: germ (the nutrients), the endosperm (starch), and the bran (the outer covering of the grain and source of fiber). Whole grains contain all these parts. Refined grains have had most of the germ and the bran removed. Enriched grains are refined grains with added vitamins (usually the B vitamins). Whole grains are desirable because they supply us with complex carbohydrates, soluble and insoluble fiber, vitamins-B and -E, minerals such as iron, zinc and magnesium, and some protein. Grains are low in fat and sodium and contain no cholesterol.

COOKING TIMES FOR GRAINS

Boiling and simmering in a seasoned broth or water is the preferred method of cooking all grains. The grains are either added directly to the boiling liquid, or first toasted then added. The chart gives amount of liquid and cooking time for 1 cup of grain. In the recipes that follow, one grain may be substituted for another. Just be certain to adjust cooking time.

GRAIN (1 CUP)	LIQUID	COOKING TIME
hulled barley (not pearl)	3 cups	1 hour and 15 minutes
brown rice	2½ cups	45 minutes
converted rice	2 cups	18 minutes
bulgur	2 cups	15 minutes
millet	2½ cups	20 minutes
quinoa	2 cups	15 minutes
wheat berries	2 cups	45 minutes to 1 hour

STORAGE

Store uncooked grains in air-tight containers in a cool, dry space. Cooked grains may be kept in the refrigerator for 3 to 4 days; 6 to 8 weeks in the freezer.

RED AND GREEN BAKED BARLEY

Servings: 4

Hulled barley has only the inedible hull removed; pot or Scotch barley has only small amounts of of the bran removed; pearl barley has had almost all of the bran and germ removed. To speed up the cooking time for hulled barley, soak it overnight in water. For pearl barley decrease the cooking time in this recipe to 45 minutes.

1 cup hulled or Scotch barley
1 medium onion, finely chopped
2–3 cloves garlic, minced or mashed
1/2 cup finely chopped parsley
2 medium tomatoes, coarsely chopped or 1/4 cup chopped dried tomatoes
2 cups unsalted, defatted chicken or vegetable stock

Heat oven to 350º. In a 4-cup casserole pan with a tight fitting lid, combine barley, onion, garlic, parsley, tomatoes and stock. Bake for 1 1/2 hours or until barley is soft.

per serving *207 calories, 6 g protein, 58.8 g carb., 1.1 mg cholesterol, 16 mg sodium*

WARM BARLEY PUDDING

Barley was brought to the New World by Dutch and British colonists so that they could continue making beer. Malt syrup, made from sprouted barley, is the magic ingredient. Barley malt can be found in specialty food stores. It's use is not limited to beer.

2 cups hulled or Scotch barley
6 cups nonfat milk
1 cup chopped dried fruit (raisins, apples, pears)
3/4 cup all-fruit sweetener or 1/4 cup barley malt
1 cup fruit-flavored, nonfat milk

Preheat oven to 325°. Combine barley, milk, dried fruit and fruit sweetener ina 6-cup casserole with a tight fitting lid. Bake for about 2 hours or until milk is absorbed and barley is soft. Serve warm, topped with flavored yogurt.

per serving *552 calories, 19.5 g protein, 121 g carb., 1.7 g fat, 5 mg chol, 173 g sodium*

MILLET AND PEAR PUDDING

Thanks to Goldie Caughlan, Nutrition Educator at Puget Consumer Co-op in Seattle, Washington for giving us permission to use this delicious recipe. She says it is a no-fail recipe; if the mixture seems too thin, cook longer; if too thick add more liquid.

1 1/2 cups apple juice
1/2 cup millet
1 large pear, chopped into bite-sized pieces
1/4 cup raisins or currants
1 tsp. cinnamon
2 tbs. pumpkin seeds
nonfat milk

Pour apple juice into a medium saucepan; bring to a boil. Add millet, pears raisins and cinnamon; reduce heat, cover and simmer about 20 minutes. Sprinkle cooked pudding with seeds and serve with milk.

per serving without milk *126 calories, 1.5 g protein, 30 g carb., 0.9 g fat, 0 mg cholesterol, 5 g sodium*

CRUNCHY BROWN RICE

Either short-grain or long-grain rice may be used in this cooked rice dish. The big difference is that short-grain rice cooks up sticky and long-grain rice comes out fluffy.

$2^{1}/_{2}$ cups unsalted, defatted chicken or vegetable stock
3–4 green onions including tops, chopped
1 cup brown rice
1 medium tomato, chopped
$^{1}/_{4}$ cup fresh or frozen corn
2–4 tbs. canned diced green chiles
1 tbs. unsalted Dijon-style mustard
$^{1}/_{4}$ cup chopped water chestnuts

In a large saucepan, combine stock and green onions, bring to a boil and add rice. Reduce heat, cover and simmer 45 minutes. Uncover pan and stir in tomato, corn, green chiles, mustard and chestnuts. Serve warm.

per serving 208 calories, 5 g protein, 59.9 g carb., 2.1 g fat., 1 mg cholesterol, 113 mg sodium

BASMATI RICE SALAD

Brown basmati rice is not a new rice, but only in the last few years has it appeared on supermarket shelves. Popular in India for years, where its name means "queen of fragrance," basmati rice has a distinctive nutty flavor and is reputed to have fewer calories than other long-grain rice. You can use ordinary rice or any grain for this recipe, but do give basmati or texmati, the American equivalent a try.

2 cups cooked, browned basmati or texmati rice
1 red or yellow bell pepper, chopped
2 small tomatoes, chopped
4 black olives, pitted and chopped
1/2 cup currants

1 cup fresh or frozen peas, thawed
1/2 cup low-fat ricotta cheese
1/4 cup plain, nonfat yogurt
1 tbs. unsalted Dijon-style mustard
freshly ground black pepper to taste

In a medium salad bowl, combine rice, pepper, tomatoes, olives, currants and peas. In a food processor or blender, purée ricotta cheese, yogurt and mustard. Toss cheese mixture with rice and vegetables. Season with pepper and store covered in the refrigerator until served.

per serving *222 calories, 9.9 g protein, 37 g carb., 4.4 g fat, 10 mg cholesterol, 150 mg sodium*

QUINOA PILAF

Quinoa (keen-wa) has an excellent balance of amino acids which gives it a high protein rating. Couple that with ample amounts of vitamins, minerals and fiber, and the fact that quinoa cooks in 15 minutes, and you can see why quinoa gets high marks from nutritionist. Quinoa must be rinsed before cooking to remove the "saporin" that covers the seeds. Tahini is sesame seed paste, often used in Middle Eastern cooking and found in most grocery stores.

2 cups plus 2 tbs. unsalted, defatted chicken or vegetable stock or nonstick cooking spray
1 small onion, finely chopped
1 tart apple, finely chopped

1 tsp. low-sodium soy sauce
1 cup quinoa, rinsed
1 tbs. tahini, no salt added
2 tsp. toasted sesame seeds

Heat 2 tbs. stock in a nonstick skillet or lightly coat pan with nonstick spray. Add onion and cook until soft; add apple and soy sauce. Add remaining stock and bring to a boil; add quinoa. Reduce heat, cover and simmer about 15 minutes. Uncover, fluff grain and stir in tahini and sesame seeds.

per serving *165 calories, 5.8 g protein, 40 g carb., 3.3 g fat, 1 mg cholesterol, 3 mg sodium*

CREAMY GRAIN BERRY SALAD WITH FRUIT

Servings: 4

Wheat berries are the seeds of the wheat plant. They are what the mills grind to make flour. We like to toss them in salads, soups and casseroles. When cooking wheat berries or other grains for a fruit salad, use fruit juice instead of water for the liquid.

2 cups cooked wheat berries
1 cup chopped jicama
1 large apple, cut into bite-sized pieces
1 orange, cut into bite-sized pieces
1 cup low-fat ricotta cheese

1/4 cup all-fruit sweetener
1 tsp. cinnamon
1/2 tsp. cardamom
1/4 chopped dates

In a large salad bowl, combine wheat berries, jicama, apple and orange. In a small bowl mix together ricotta cheese, fruit sweetener, cinnamon, cardamom and dates. Toss with berries and fruit. Cover and refrigerate until served.

per serving *234 calories, 10.3 g protein, 0 g carb., 5.4 g fat, 19 mg cholesterol, 80 mg sodium*

DESSERTS

139 Fresh Fruit Presentations
140 Warm and Cozy Baked Fruit
141 Ginger Peachy Bread Pudding
142 That Chocolate Thing
143 Fruit Gelatin

144 Fourth of July Fruitcake
145 Baked Apricot Snow
146 Tri-Berry Trifle
148 Fruit Crisp
149 Poached Pears With Berry Sauce

Whoever said a good dessert had to be sinful? A fruit dish created with imagination can satisfy anyone's craving to end the meal with something sweet. Fruits naturally contain lots of sugar, so they don't need additional sweetening. In fact, fruit or fruit juice concentrates can be the sweetening agent for other food products, so you can still have desserts that are creamy cold concoctions or fragrant baked puddings. Canned and dried fruits work well, too; just be sure that the canned fruit has been canned in fruit juices, without added sugar.

FRESH FRUIT PRESENTATIONS

BUFFET

Arrange a variety of bite-size chunks of fruit—fresh, frozen or canned in juice—on a serving platter. Provide a bowl of dip and toothpicks. Use our *Creamy Yogurt Sauce* (below), applesauce colored with cherry or raspberry purée, or Wax Orchard's brand fruit-sweetened Fudge Sweet or Ginger Sweet sauces, both made without fat.

FRUIT SALAD

The same variety of fruits, but with a dollop of sauce spooned over individual servings.

CREAMY YOGURT SAUCE

1 cup plain, nonfat yogurt
3 tbs. all-fruit sweetener

1/4 tsp. ground cinnamon

Mix all ingredients together. Chill several hours for flavors to blend.

---

per tablespoon *13 calories, 0.9 g protein, 2/4 g carb., 0 g fat, 0 mg cholesterol, 11 mg sodium*

WARM AND COZY BAKED FRUIT

Change the combination of fruit and the flavors of spread and juice to make unending variations of our favorite winter preparation.

2 large apples, cored and sliced
1 large or 2 small winter pears, cored and sliced
2 bananas, peeled and sliced
1 tbs. fruit juice-sweetened marmalade
4 tbs. orange juice
1 cup plain, nonfat yogurt, optional

Heat oven to 375°. In an 8-inch nonstick baking dish or one that has been sprayed with nonstick spray, arrange slices of apples, pears and bananas. Combine marmalade and juice, and drizzle over fruit. Cover tightly with foil. Bake 20 minutes. Serve topped with a dollop of yogurt if desired.

per serving without yogurt 91 calories, 2.1 g protein, 21.5 g carb., 0.4 g fat, 1 mg cholesterol, 23 mg sodium

GINGER PEACHY BREAD PUDDING

Servings: 8

For friends who don't eat meat, and friends who don't eat dairy products: another warm and cozy dessert that is so good for you, it's a nutritionist's dream!

1 can (1 lb.) peaches in fruit juices
4 cups cubed, whole wheat bread
1/2 lb. tofu drained, pressed and cubed
2 tbs. all-fruit sweetener

3 tsp. grated fresh ginger or 1 tsp. ground
  ginger
1/2 tsp. vanilla
reduced-fat egg product equal to 1 egg
1/4 cup golden raisins

Heat oven to 350°. Pour juice from peaches into a food processor or blender, and cut peaches into bite-sized pieces. In a large bowl, combine bread cubes and peaches. In a food processor, combine juice with tofu, sweetener, ginger, vanilla and egg product. Process until smooth. Pour over bread cubes and mix well. Stir in raisins. Turn into a 9-inch nonstick baking pan or one coated with nonstick spray. Bake for 30 minutes, or until top is brown and crusty, and a toothpick inserted in center comes out clean.

per serving *161 calories, 7.4 g protein, 28.5 g carb., 3.3 g fat, 1 mg cholesterol, 204 mg sodium*

THAT CHOCOLATE THING

Cold, it's something like a brownie. Warm, it's a cakelike pudding. Either way, your friends won't believe it's a low-fat dessert!

1 cup low-fat ricotta cheese
2/3 cup all-fruit sweetener
1 tsp. vanilla
3/4 cup all-purpose flour

3 tbs. Dutch-process cocoa
1 tsp. baking powder
reduced-fat egg product equal to 3 eggs

Heat oven to 350°. In a medium bowl, combine ricotta, sweetener and vanilla. Set aside for 10 minutes. In another bowl, combine flour, cocoa and baking powder. Stir egg product into ricotta mix, and then add flour mix. Blend well, and turn into an 8-or-9-inch square baking pan that has been coated with nonstick spray. Bake for 25–30 minutes, or until a toothpick inserted in the center comes out clean.

per serving *294 calories, 16.9 g protein, 41.3 g carb., 7.5 g fat, 19 mg cholesterol, 191 mg sodium*

FRUIT GELATIN

In many homes, for many children, gelatin, either cut in plain squares or with pieces of fruit floating in clear colors, is still the dessert of choice. Commercial pre-sweetened gelatin is 88% sugar. Who needs it, when it's just as easy to make your own fruit gelatin?

1/2 cup water
1 1/2 cups fruit juice of your choice
1 envelope unflavored gelatin
1–2 tsp. all-fruit sweetener, optional
1 cup cut fresh or frozen fruit (except pineapple)

In a small saucepan, combine water, juice, gelatin and sweetener. Stir over low heat until gelatin is completely dissolved. Pour into a bowl and chill until gelatin is cool and syrupy. Stir in fruit and chill until firm, about 3 hours.

per serving *68 calories, 2.2 g protein, 14,9 g carb., 0.3 g fat, 0 mg cholesterol, 3 mg sodium*

FOURTH OF JULY FRUIT CAKE

Servings: 8

Serve this red, white and blue confection before fireworks.

2 envelopes unflavored gelatin
2^1/$_2$ cups white grape juice
2 cinnamon sticks, each 1–2 inches long
1 cup nonfat sour cream or plain, nonfat yogurt
1–3 tbs. all-fruit sweetener, depending on sweetness of fruit
1 cup fresh frozen blueberries
1 cup fresh frozen raspberries or strawberries

Soften gelatin in ^{1}/$_2$ cup juice. Set aside. In a small saucepan, combine remaining juice, cinnamon sticks and sweetener. Bring to a boil and simmer 5 minutes. Remove cinnamon sticks. Blend in softened gelatin and sour cream or nonfat yogurt. Chill until mixture begins to thicken. Fold in fruits and pour into deep glass bowl or into a 4-cup mold. Chill until firm.

per serving *91 calories, 3.9 g protein, 19.1 g carb., 0.3 g fat, 1 mg cholesterol, 27 mg sodium*

BAKED APRICOT SNOW

Servings: 6

Because the original version of this dessert used uncooked egg whites, we were afraid we would have to cut it from the book. (New standards tell us uncooked eggs are not safe to eat.) Then we discovered we could bake Apricot Snow, so we put it back. This dessert is scrumptious served with Wax Orchard's Fudge Sweet.

8 oz.. dried apricots
1 1/2 cups boiling water
1/3 cup all-fruit sweetener

1/2 cup orange juice
1 tbs. grated orange rind, optional
3 egg whites

In a small saucepan, cover apricots with boiling water. Set aside for 1 hour or until apricots have softened. Then simmer over medium heat 20 to 30 minutes. Purée apricots in a food processor or blender. Add sweetener, juice and orange rind to apricots. Process very briefly, just to mix. When apricots are cool, preheat oven to 275°. Beat egg whites until stiff. Fold apricots into egg whites. Pour into an 8-inch baking dish that has been sprayed with non-stick spray. Bake for 30 to 45 minutes. Serve warm or cold.

per serving *133 calories, 3.7 g protein, 32 g carb., 0.3 g fat, 0 mg cholesterol, 32 mg sodium*

TRI-BERRY TRIFLE

Angel food cake, which contains no fat at all, is a godsend to the fat-free diet. Now a new baker who makes fat-free yellow cakes has come to our town. There's a little bit of sugar in these cakes, but we feel we're entitled to an occasional splurge!

2 cups nonfat milk
2 tbs. cornstarch
2 tbs. all-fruit sweetener
reduced-fat egg product equal to 2 eggs
1 tsp. vanilla
1 (12 oz.) packaged angel food or other fat-free cake
4 tbs. all fruit raspberry spread
1/2 cup sweet sherry, or substitute 1/2 cup apple juice
2 cups fresh or frozen combined raspberries, strawberries and blueberries

In a small saucepan, combine milk, cornstarch and sweetener. Cook over medium heat, stirring constantly, until mixture comes to a boil and thickens. In a small bowl, stir a small amount of hot milk into egg substitute; return to saucepan. Bring to boil again, stirring and cook for 1 minute. Remove from heat and stir in vanilla. Set in a bowl of ice to cool.

While mixture cools, cut cake into 1-inch thick slices. Spread with raspberry spread. Arrange cake, spread side up, along bottom and up sides of a deep 8-or-9-inch straight-sided glass bowl. Cut extra cake into cubes and scatter in bowl. Drizzle sherry over all. Set aside for flavors to blend.

About 2 hours before serving, scatter berries over cake. Check cooled custard for lumps; if necessary, strain custard. Pour custard over berries and serve.

per serving *197 calories, 7.4 g protein, 36.3 g carb., 0.9 g fat, 1 mg cholesterol, 181 mg sodium*

FRUIT CRISP

To be certain whole wheat bread crumb topping gives you all the nutritional value that it should, check the list of ingredients on the bread you buy. The first one should be whole wheat flour.

1 cup whole wheat bread crumbs (about 2 slices)
1 tsp. cinnamon
3 tbs. all-fruit sweetener
3 cups Italian plum halves or 3 cups pitted cherries
1–2 tbs. additional all-fruit sweetener, optional
1 cup plain, nonfat yogurt, optional

Heat oven to 375°. Mix crumbs with cinnamon and sweetener. Pat half the crumbs into the bottom of a 9-inch baking pan that has been sprayed with nonstick spray. Taste fruit; if fruit is too tart, stir with additional sweetener. Arrange fruit on crumbs, plums cut side down. Top with remaining crumbs. Bake for 30 minutes, until brown and crisp. Serve with a dollop of yogurt if desired.

per serving *114 calories, 4.33 g protein, 23,7 g carb., 1 g fat, 1 mg cholesterol, 92 mg sodium*

POACHED PEARS WITH BERRY SAUCE

Top each pear with low-fat ricotta cheese that has been flavored with poaching liquid.

2 medium-sized firm pears, halved and
  cored
1 cup pineapple juice
$1/2$ cup water
1 tsp. vanilla

1 cup fresh or frozen raspberries
1 tbs. orange liqueur, optional
2 tbs. pineapple juice concentrate
Ricotta cheese, optional

Place pears in a pan large enough to hold them without touching. Combine pineapple juice, water, lemon juice and vanilla; pour over pears. Simmer covered for 15 minutes or until pears are soft but not mushy. Remove pears to serving platter. Reduce liquid until syrupy. Spoon over pears. At serving time purée berries with liqueur and juice concentrate. Spoon over pears. Top with ricotta cheese if desired.

per serving *116 calories, 2.7 g protein, 22.7 g carb., 1.6 g fat, 5 mg cholesterol, 21 mg sodium*

A NOTE ON THE NUTRITIONAL INFORMATION

The nutritional analysis that follows each recipe in this book was prepared by the publisher using a computer program called *THE FOOD PROCESSOR II, NUTRITION AND DIET ANALYSIS SYSTEM**, which is based on data from the United States Department of Agriculture and many other resources. Readers should understand that these figures are only approximate. For example, the analysis of chicken recipes assumes 4 ounces of lean breast chicken, skin removed, per serving. However, a skinless half chicken breast may vary in weight from 3 to 6 ounces; that same chicken breast may have more or less fat clinging to it, depending on the diligence of the cook who removed the skin. Also, the computer bases its analysis on an average of a number of different products; you may find in your own market foods with differing amounts of fat, sodium and sugar. The pita bread in FOOD PROCESSOR II contains 339 milligrams of sodium; we have found one brand in our local area that has only 120 milligrams.

The sodium content of some of the recipes may seem high in a book that calls itself "no salt." Although the authors make a point of seeking out products that contain the lowest possible amounts of sodium, like beans canned without salt (see the list of some of our favorites, page 16), we have also chosen to use nonfat cream cheese and hard cheeses which do have significant amounts of naturally occurring sodium.

Readers should understand that the recipes in this book are not a cure or a preventative for any disease; a low-fat, low-salt diet is only one part of a daily regimen for healthy living. Questions about the role of diet in health problems should be addressed to the reader's health care provider.

*ESHA Research,P.O. Box 13028, Salem, OR 97309, or on the web at www.esha.com.

INDEX

A

Adapting recipes 16
Appetizers 20

B

Beans 51
   baked with a bite 58
   cooking times 52
   enchiladas 60
   fruit-flavored sweet 62
   garbanzo with spinach 56
   Italian-style with pasta 59
   lentils with creamy mint sauce 61
   Mexican-style 54
   pita pizza 55
   red bean salad 57
Beef 63
   Athenian market stew 64
   bulgur and meat stew 66
   Hungarian goulash 72
   meat sauce with zucchini 65

   no-fry tacos 68
   nonfat fajitas 70
   pita pies with cucumber sauce 67
   sweet and golden stew 71
Beets, baked 118
Beets, salad with corn 128
Breakfast 36
   basic omelet 48
   cereals 40–43
   Danish, low-fat cheese 44
   drinks 37–39
   muffins 50
   nonfat French toast 46
   pancakes 47
   spreads for toast 45
Browning, without fat 16

C

Cereal
   apple and oats 41
   backpackers' 43

   fat-free, sugarless granola 40
   fruit and grain 42
Cheese ball 34
Cheese, yogurt 26
Chicken 73
   braised with sun-dried tomatoes 76
   breast with orange sauce 82
   with chutney 75
   cold with mustard-tomato sauce 80
   crunchy oven-baked 81
   curried 88
   Dijonnaise 87
   Indian 78
   with mandarin oranges 89
   and potatoes 84
   simmered with peaches 85
   soup with tofu 115
   south-of-the-border style 77
   spicy with dried fruit 79
   strips with basil 74
   tortilla casserole 83

Chiles 13
Chutney, peach 33
Clams steamed in wine 103
Coleslaw, crunchy cabbage 35
Coleslaw, rosy red 121
Cream substitute 15
Curries
  apple curry dip 31
  chicken 88
  garbanzo beans with spinach 56
  Indian baked fish 92
  Indian chicken 78
  shrimp in red pepper boats 104
  shrimp salad 100

D

Danish, low-fat cheese 44
Desserts 138
  baked apricot snow 145
  Fourth of July fruitcake 143
  fresh fruit presentations 139
  fruit crisp 148
  fruit gelatin 143
  ginger peachy bread pudding 141

poached pears with berry sauce 149
that chocolate thing 142
tri-berry trifle 146
warm and cozy baked fruit 140
Dips
  apple curry 31
  creamy tofu 21
  eggplant 25
  green garden yogurt cheese 27
  herbed yogurt cheese 28
  onion-dill 30
  spicy bean 24

E

Eggs
  without cholesterol 17
  basic omelet 48
  scrambled 48
Enchiladas 60

F

Fish
  and vegetable kabobs 99
  baked with salsa 102

cold baked salmon 94
Creole baked 93
crunchy broiled 91
curried shrimp salad 100
ginger-orange steaks 96
Indian baked 92
quick and easy with orange sauce
  101
salmon mousse 95
scallops with chutney 97
shrimp curry in red pepper boats 104
spicy broiled 98
steamed clams in wine 103
French toast, nonfat 46
Fruit
  apple and oats cereal 41
  apple curry dip 31
  baked 140
  baked apricot snow 145
  berry trifle 146
  creamy grain berry salad with 137
  fresh fruit presentations 139
  fruit crisp 148
  fruitcake 144

Fruit, *continued*
   gelatin 143
   ginger peachy bread pudding 140
   and grain cereal 42
   jam 45
   peach chutney 33
   poached pears with berry sauce 149
   shakes 37–39
   soup 111

G
Grains 129
   basmati rice salad 135
   cooking times 130
   creamy grain berry salad with fruit
     137
   crunchy brown rice 134
   millet and pear pudding 133
   quinoa pilaf 136
   red and green baked barley 131
   warm barley pudding 132

J
Jam 45

M
Marinate without oil 16
Muffins, mini bran and fruit 50
Mussels, stuffed 32

O
Omelet fillings 49
Onions, baked 118

P
Pancakes 47
Pasta, Italian-style with beans 59
Pizza, bean pita 55
Products, where to buy 18,19

S
Salads
   basmati rice 135
   beet with corn 128
   red red bean 57

Salmon, cold baked 94
Salmon, mousse 95
Salsa 13
Sauce
   basic white 14
   berry 149
   creamy mint 61
   cucumber 67
   meat with zucchini 65
   salsa 13
   for vegetables 119
Sautéeing without shortening 16
Seafood 90
Shakes
   fruit 37
   orange milk shake 39
   tomato-yogurt 38
   tropical refresher 38
   yogurt 37
Shrimp curry in red pepper boats 104
Shrimp salad, curried 100
Snacks 20

Soups 105
   asparagus 114
   chicken and tofu 115
   chilled dilled 109
   cold zucchini 112
   cream 14
   frosty pumpkin bisque 113
   fruit 111
   lentil 107
   mushroom and tarragon 110
   tomato and barley 108
   vegetable 106
Spread, spicy tofu 22
Spread, white bean 23
Stew
   bulgur and meat 66
   colorful vegetable 120
   sweet and golden,beef 71
Stock, unsalted defatted chicken 8
Stock, vegetable 9

T
Taco shells, crisp 69
Tacos, no-fry 68

Tofu
   with chicken soup 115
   creamy dip 21
   spicy spread 22
   vegetable stew 120
Tomato
   sauce 10
   sauce, all-purpose 11
   stewed 12
Torta, layered cheese 29
Turkey breast with sherry 86

V
Vegetables 116
   baked beets 118
   baked onions 118
   beet salad with corn 128
   cheesy kale 125
   colorful stew 120
   cooking methods 117
   double orange sweet potatoes with
     pears 124
   marinated 122
   oven-baked chips 118

   rosy red slaw 121
   sauces for 119
   stock 9
   summer salad 123
   sweet and creamy squash 127
   tangy dressing for 119
   tomatoes 10–12
   winter casserole 126
   zesty marinade for 119

Y
Yogurt cheese 26

Serve Creative, Easy, Nutritious Meals with **nitty gritty**® Cookbooks

1 or 2, Cooking for
100 Dynamite Desserts
9 x 13 Pan Cookbook
Bagels, Best
Barbecue Cookbook
Beer and Good Food
Big Book of Bread Machine Recipes
Big Book of Kitchen Appliance Recipes
Big Book of Snacks and Appetizers
Blender Drinks
Bread Baking
Bread Machine
Bread Machine II
Bread Machine III
Bread Machine V
Bread Machine VI
Bread Machine, Entrees
Burger Bible
Cappuccino/Espresso
Casseroles
Chicken, Unbeatable
Chile Peppers
Clay, Cooking in

Coffee and Tea
Convection Oven
Cook-Ahead Cookbook
Crockery Pot, Extra-Special
Deep Fryer
Dehydrator Cookbook
Edible Gifts
Edible Pockets
Fabulous Fiber Cookery
Fondue and Hot Dips
Fondue, New International
Freezer, 'Fridge, Pantry
Garlic Cookbook
Grains, Cooking with
Healthy Cooking on Run
Ice Cream Maker
Indoor Grill, Cooking on
Italian Recipes, Quick and Easy
Juicer Book II
Kids, Cooking with Your
Kids, Healthy Snacks for
Loaf Pan, Recipes for
Low-Carb Recipes

Lowfat American
No Salt No Sugar No Fat   (REVISED)
Party Foods/Appetizers
Pasta Machine Cookbook
Pasta, Quick and Easy
Pinch of Time
Pizza, Best
Porcelain, Cooking in
Pressure Cooker, Recipes (REVISED)
Rice Cooker
Rotisserie Oven Cooking
Sandwich Maker
Simple Substitutions
Skillet, Sensational
Slow Cooking
Slow Cooker, Vegetarian
Soups and Stews
Soy & Tofu Recipes
Tapas Fantásticas
Toaster Oven Cookbook
Waffles & Pizzelles
Wedding Catering Cookbook
Wraps and Roll-Ups   (REVISED)

For a free catalog, call: Bristol Publishing Enterprises
(800) 346-4889
www.bristolpublishing.com